Praise for *Storms Can't Hurt the Sky*

"Cohen's compelling account of the dissolution of his marriage illustrates important Buddhist teachings—and offers valuable advice on how these teachings can ease the pain for anyone undergoing this critical transition."

— Susan Piver, meditation teacher, author of *How Not to Be Afraid of Your Own Life* and *The Hard Questions*

"In clear, propulsive prose, Cohen bravely revisits his own divorce and shares the Buddhist teachings that helped him through it. The book is both an act of forgiveness and a plea for same. This is a real page-turner."

— Virginia Vitzthum, former Salon.com columnist and author of *I Love You, Let's Meet: Adventures in Online Dating*

"This is a great addition to the tool kit that everyone needs when they get divorced. Well done!"

— Katherine Lanpher, author of *Leap Days* and a contributing editor at *More* magazine

Storms Can't Hurt the Sky

Also by Gabriel Cohen

Red Hook

Boombox

The Graving Dock

Storms Can't Hurt the Sky

A Buddhist Path Through Divorce

Gabriel Cohen

Da Capo Lifelong
A Member of the Perseus Books Group

"I Still Miss Someone"
Words and Music by Johnny Cash and Roy Cash Jr.
©1958 (renewed) Unichappell Music Inc. All rights reserved.
Used by permission of Alfred Publishing Co., Inc.

Designed by Linda Mark
Set in 11.5 point Cochin by the Perseus Books Group

Cataloging-in-Publication data for this book is available from the Library of Congress.
First Da Capo Press edition 2008
ISBN-10: 1-60094-050-1
ISBN-13: 978-1-60094-050-7

Published by Da Capo Press
A Member of the Perseus Books Group
www.dacapopress.com

Da Capo Press books are available at special discounts for bulk purchases in the United States by corporations, institutions, and other organizations. For more information, please contact the Special Markets Department at the Perseus Books Group, 2300 Chestnut Street, Suite 200, Philadelphia, PA 19103, or call (800) 255-1514, or e-mail special.markets@perseusbooks.com.

1 2 3 4 5 6 7 8 9

For J.

contents

part three: arrows into flowers

introduction

At seven in the evening on June 25, 2005, my wife suddenly got up and walked out the door.

She never came back.

It was the worst thing that ever happened to me.

It was also, oddly enough, one of the best.

That calamity sent me scrambling for new meaning in life, and I found it in the last place I would ever have imagined.

What I learned astonished me: that change and loss are inevitable, but that the suffering we derive from them is not. That insight enabled me to get through some brutally tough times.

⌐

I've been a writer for a while. Back in the mid-eighties I wrote an article about a program founded by Dr. Bernie Siegel, author of a bestseller called *Love, Medicine and Miracles.*

He ran support groups for patients with cancer or other life-threatening illnesses.

Some of them said that they considered their diseases a gift.

Some of them were dying at the time.

In an abstract way, I could understand their point. Their crises gave them a new perspective on what was important in life. They learned to spend less time watching TV sitcoms, more time repairing relationships with their loved ones. Less time worrying about career advancement, more time enjoying their kids. They didn't waste time because they didn't have time to waste.

Did I change *my* life as a result of talking to those people? No. I still ate junk food and wasted precious hours watching TV. I burned up lots of time worrying about my career. I let important relationships deteriorate or fall by the wayside.

Decades passed.

When my own personal crisis struck, all my writerly detachment went up in smoke. All of a sudden, the issue of suffering was no longer abstract. And things quickly got worse. Not only was the love of my life gone, but I had recently been informed that the house in which I had been renting an apartment for sixteen years was about to be sold; I could only pray that I would be able to find an affordable new home on my own. I craved emotional support, but found that when I needed them most, friends I had shared with my spouse disappeared from my life without a word of sympathy or kindness. (That's common in divorce, but I didn't know that at the time.) In the weeks and months that followed, there were times when I felt like I was being flayed alive.

I desperately needed help.

Luckily, I found it.

♌

As a part-time journalist and full-time New Yorker, my sense of skepticism is pretty well developed. I certainly didn't expect that *Buddhism* would have something to offer me. Yeah, the Dalai Lama seems like a pretty cool guy, and the idea of peace and serenity certainly sounded good, especially when my marriage was blowing up, but ever since I lived through the sixties as a kid, I have always been wary of New Age grooviness and mumbo-jumbo. What little I knew about Buddhism was colored by all sorts of popular misconceptions. When I was young, I watched the TV show *Kung Fu*—remember its Shaolin monks spouting vague Buddhist philosophy? More recently, I had seen Buddhism portrayed as a fad for rock stars and Hollywood actors.

But when my marriage was in its final throes, I stumbled across a Buddhist lecture. I expected foreign prayers and remote ritual, but was greatly surprised: the talk was down-to-earth and very relevant to what I was going through. Instead of an esoteric religion, I found a helpful new way to look at my everyday life.

What does Buddhism have to do with divorce? The answer is surprisingly simple and direct. Marriage is a search for happiness. Divorce is all about how that search can sour into suffering. What is the fundamental, root subject of Buddhism? *Everyone wants two things: to avoid suffering, and to find happiness.* Buddhism is more than a set of beliefs—it's a practical method for becoming happier and suffering less.

If I became a slightly kinder person as a result of my troubles, if I mended some bridges with family and friends, if I learned to smell a few more roses—all of that would have been swell. What I discovered, though, was much bigger. My wake-up call led me to a new understanding of how life works.

❏

We're not talking about a lone search for enlightenment here.

Sure, it must be hard to be a single monk hidden away on retreat, renouncing all life's pleasures. But isn't it just as challenging to live the life of a normal married or divorced person? Sharing all of life's difficulties with someone over a period of years, or trying to preserve some sort of amicable relationship over the course of a difficult breakup—these are major spiritual tests. (Thankfully, my wife and I didn't have kids—I can only imagine how hard it would be to stay calm if the person I once loved was trying to deny me shared custody of my own child.)

Any two people in intimate contact find themselves in an intense spiritual arena. In the middle of a difficult marriage or divorce, that arena is liable to be filled with flying arrows. And both sides are going to get wounded.

If you're in that perilous situation right now, I'm going to assume that you're seeking more than just abstract insights. You want protection. You want relief. You want *help*.

As we move through this book, we're going to do five basic things:

We're going to examine how the happiness of marriage can change into the suffering of divorce.

We're going to look at where we believe that suffering comes from.

We're going to take a surprising look at where it *really* comes from.

We're going to learn how to actively change our experience of breakups or divorce—how to make them less damaging and traumatic.

Finally, we'll discover how to use the suffering of a failed relationship as a springboard that can help us move on toward a more stable, lasting peace and happiness, especially when a new relationship comes along.

At this point I'll just note that Yes, this is a book about Buddhism, but I have no vested interest in trying to convert anyone. (I don't get trading stamps for signing people up.) Because Buddhism is not a god-based religion, it doesn't have to conflict with your current religious or scientific beliefs. This book may motivate you to learn more about Buddhism, or it may not. That's your business. All I want is to help you deal with the pain of a difficult relationship.

I'm not a Tibetan lama or a lifelong meditation guru, and I can't expound on esoteric Buddhist teachings, but I know what it's like to go through a painful divorce. And I've done a lot of research, interviewed other divorced people, and gathered insights from people who *are* experts about Buddhism, as well as psychology and social science. I'm going to describe what helped me, and introduce some powerful ideas that may help you.

A shocking percentage of modern marriages will end in divorce. If you're on the painful end of that statistic, I believe that what I learned might be of real support and sustenance to you.

As a matter of fact, you may find the ideas in this book helpful in many areas of your life, and a source of solace if you're suffering from any change or loss.

AUTHOR'S NOTE: Many of the names in the following account have been changed.

part one

A WAKE-UP CALL

punching holes

These first few chapters will begin with anger and end with a murder. Along the way, I'll begin to introduce the possibility of a life free of suffering—for me, for you, and for everybody else in the world.

Then we'll break for lunch.

♩

I don't think of myself as a particularly angry person. I have rarely demonstrated anger in any physical way. The only time I can remember getting in a fistfight was in sixth grade, when a bully pushed things too far and we took a few wild swings at each other after school one day.

In the darkest moments of my marriage I never contemplated doing any kind of physical harm.

But as things deteriorated, I got angry. Big time.

An apartment search may seem like a trivial thing to fight about, but studies have shown that having to move is one of the most stressful challenges that a couple can face. It was especially trying in the New York real estate market, where rents were going through the roof, where struggling artists like myself and my wife were continually being pushed into farther reaches of the city by a relentless process of gentrification.

I had been terribly spoiled. When I first moved to New York, I found a small but likeable Brooklyn apartment for an impossibly low rent. At that time, the neighborhood was plain and dull compared to glamorous Manhattan next door, but it had its charms. I had access to a garden with a fig tree and a rusty swing seat, in the midst of a green courtyard. My landlord was a kind old Italian-American man; he raised the rent only twice in sixteen years.

Twelve years into my stay, my future wife—I'll call her Claire—moved in with me.

We had met when she came from Denver to visit some mutual friends. I first saw her at a dinner in a funky little restaurant in Chinatown. She was beautiful (like the subject of a Modigliani portrait) and smart and talented and sweet, and I soon developed a powerful crush. She was in town for five days, and although we spent four of those days together, I didn't know how she felt about me until the last night of her stay. We had dinner at our friends' apartment; as the evening wore on, I still couldn't tell if my attraction was returned. At one in the morning, another guest called a car service to go home. Reluctantly, I offered to share the ride. The car came. I went out into the hallway and Claire came out to say goodbye. We hugged, and the hug turned into a kiss, and the kiss turned increasingly passionate, and then I went out into the street and told the car service to leave without me.

Claire had to leave the next morning, but we kept in touch by phone for the next couple of weeks. I was completely smitten. I felt so strongly about her that I made her a mix tape of unabashed love songs, including the Temptations singing "My Girl," a song we had listened to during the taxi ride to the airport. I soon flew out to Denver to see her on a blizzardy New Year's Eve. We spent blissful nights under her big down comforter, while it snowed and snowed outside. Within just a few days, I told her that I was falling in love. She said she felt the same. I had planned to visit for a week, but ended up staying a month. I was thirty-nine and had been through a number of relationships, but I sensed early on that this was *the one* — that my lifelong search for a true romantic partner had finally, happily, reached its end. For the next eight months, we kept up a whirlwind long-distance romance, meeting at a wedding in New Orleans, her sister's house in Chicago, a friend's place out in Washington State. The culmination of our courtship was a major test: Claire had a summer job as a fire lookout in Arizona. I joined her and we lived together in one fourteen-square-foot room, on top of a rugged mountain, with no electricity or hot water, completely isolated from the rest of the world. We figured that if we could get along through that, we could get through anything.

We had a great time.

Claire moved in with me on September 1, 2001: *Welcome to New York*. Ten days later, the World Trade Center came down. We went out that morning and tried to donate blood, and then we simply huddled in bed together, staring in shock at the TV. One week later, I found my landlord lying on his kitchen floor upstairs; he had suffered a powerful stroke. He was fiercely independent, but he could no longer look after himself, so off he went to stay with relatives in the Midwest. Claire and I had the house to ourselves.

Compared to all that drama, a mere apartment search should have seemed like a walk in the park.

In my time in New York I had heard of couples being pushed to divorce by the trial of relocation, and even heard of couples who had broken up but continued to live together because neither party could afford to move. But those were other people.

I remember how I felt on our wedding day, when I watched the love of my life walk down the aisle. We had planned a magical ceremony. It took place on a rocky pier on the Brooklyn waterfront, with New York harbor and the Statue of Liberty as backdrop. The afternoon started out gray, but just before the ceremony the sun came out, glorious. I walked out first with the wedding party, accompanied by a small marching band: a drummer, a violinist, and an accordion player. I stood there in my new suit, waiting anxiously for Claire to appear. I worked part-time as a staff supervisor for catering companies, and I had watched hundreds of weddings, and so I might have expected to be a bit blasè about this moment, but when the little flower girl appeared, and then I saw Claire gliding toward me, so stunning, resplendent in her wedding dress, I couldn't help it: I was flooded with love for her and I choked up.

We rarely fought, or even argued. We had the kind of relationship in which we told each other that we were best friends, said *I love you* at least once a day, gave each other massages at night. We were talking about when to have kids. For one Valentine's Day, I built her a box filled with a collage of mementos from our time together. On the cover, I glued two pictures of rocking chairs, which represented how

I looked forward to growing old with her. We shared the kind of fairytale romance that made other people jealous, as a shocked coworker of my wife's told me when she heard of our impending divorce.

We had four years in our little love nest, with its charming old wallpaper, its bright garden. Eventually, though, the cost of taking care of my landlord became too much for his relatives. At the same time, New York entered into a real estate frenzy, and the value of the house skyrocketed. (No doubt the old man would have had a second stroke to learn that his crumbling, lopsided brick row house was now priced at a million dollars.) One result was inevitable: my wife and I would not be able to hold onto our home.

When we started looking at apartments, we found that we disagreed about everything: how many rooms we needed, what neighborhoods to look in, how much we could afford. For the first time in our marriage, we began to have big fights.

Our union clearly did not end just because of disagreements about where to live. There was no obvious single cause—no infidelities, no physical abuse, no one action by either party that could explain why it fell apart. Like any relationship, it was a complicated two-sided story, with lots of personal history lurking in the background. Having to move exposed hidden fault lines and subjected them to unbearable pressure.

I was having some issues with my parents and Claire got caught in the middle. And she brought an untrained dog to our marriage that I couldn't get along with; I was trying to write in a small apartment and the nervous, constantly barking animal drove me nuts. Eventually, my wife very generously gave it away into the care of some friends, but my inability to accept her pet was deeply distressing to her.

On the other hand, in the middle of our marriage a certain financial situation arose, and the way Claire chose to handle it was deeply distressing to me—I felt wounded by what I interpreted as a lack of concern about our mutual welfare. It hurt my masculine pride to bring the subject up, so I just nursed my sense of injury in silence.

Did the marriage end because of *those* difficulties? I don't think so, but they certainly signaled that our fairytale romance was not so perfect after all. I think we both began to ask ourselves: what happened to the ideal spouse I thought I married? For each of us, the person who had seemed like the greatest cause of our happiness was somehow starting to seem like an obstacle to it.

I grew agitated, confused, and depressed, and I did a lousy job of managing my frustration and anger. I remember one argument in which I got so upset that I shouted full force at Claire, jumped up, stormed out of the room, and slammed the door. My anger was a sudden flare, so harsh and hot that it temporarily drove all love for her out of my heart. My outburst clearly pained Claire, and it even surprised me. I was a generally cheerful person with a goofy sense of humor, prone to doing bad impressions of JFK or characters from *The Simpsons*. Suddenly I was transformed into the Incredible Hulk.

◯

Our arguments continued, and grew stronger. It became increasingly obvious that Claire and I had very different approaches to life. We made several joint visits to therapists, but somehow—like an airplane with failing engines—our marriage seemed locked into a downward spiral. Our sex life suffered, then became nonexistent.

One day not long before our apartment deadline, I was in such despair that I wondered—aloud, unfortunately—if Claire and I might be better off going our separate ways. Under normal circumstances, it would have been the kind of stupid thing you say in the heat of the moment, regret and apologize for, and then kiss and make up.

But five minutes later she stood up and walked out.

I didn't call out, didn't follow her to the door. I just lay down on the couch with one arm draped over my face, as if I was settling into the coffin of our marriage, until dusk closed in and the room went dark.

For the first few days after Claire left, I actually didn't feel too bad. I was in a major state of shock and denial. *She'll get tired of sleeping on her friends' sofas*, I told myself. *She'll realize that we were just going through a rough patch. When she cools off, she'll come back and we can start working things out.*

After she had been gone long enough for real worry to set in, I started asking if we could talk, but she said that her mind was made up: our marriage was over. I was stunned. We had given each other a vow. *Through good times and bad times, through thick and through thin.* She couldn't possibly abandon that because of a few difficult months. I couldn't imagine that I deserved such cold treatment. I had never cheated on her, or drank to excess, or done so many of the crummy things that can make a marriage fail. And I certainly loved her.

After a number of further attempts to try to talk, I stopped reaching out. The pain of her rejection was so intense that I was afraid to risk more.

If "hope," as Emily Dickinson wrote, "is the thing with feathers," I remember the exact moment when the feathers fell off. After Claire had been gone almost a month, she called to say that she wanted to talk. My heart soared, but the conversation did not go well. She didn't want to discuss anything; she just wanted to tell me—out of the blue—that she had signed a lease on a new apartment.

I felt like I had been stabbed.

And I finally realized that I was on my own. The clock was ticking; I had only a month left before I had to leave our apartment. That place meant a lot to me. Not only had I spent sixteen years living in it, but I worked mostly at home. I had written my novels there, the ones that never got published and then one that finally did. Those rooms surrounded me like a protective shell; they felt like an extension of my self. But I had no choice; I had to go.

Stunned and alone, I headed out into the crazy New York real estate market. I could no longer afford to live in my old neighborhood; I would have to look farther afield, in alien areas, places that would mean longer commutes and unfamiliar trains. The first apartment I looked at was underground. A one-bedroom with two small casement windows, it was marked by some disco-era tenant: a wall-size photomural of Manhattan at night, a frosted Plexiglas bar with fluorescent lights shining from within. Above the apartment was a doctor's office: Adolescent Gynecology. I pressed on. Some brokers, I soon learned, routinely lied. One guy's "Lovely, Spacious Studio" turned out to be a cave the size of a walk-in closet; it looked out on a grimy airshaft. I started looking at ads for shares. "Woman seeks roommate," read one. "I am mid-60s, clinically depressed. Touch my computer and I will kill you." That was followed by a little smiley face.

I kept looking, beginning to panic that I would end up on the street. Between broker appointments, I mourned my marriage. When I wasn't grieving, I raged at Claire's betrayal of my commitment and trust. One weekend, I went out of town so she could come back and move all her things. When I returned, I took a stunned tour of the hollow shell of what had been our home.

I'll never forget the moment I hit rock bottom. In the middle of a brutal summer heat wave, the kind where the city asphalt actually begins to melt, I was walking down Brooklyn's Avenue C, my shirt soaked with sweat. I had just looked at another dingy, overpriced little studio apartment, had just been turned down by another building manager because my freelancer's income was hard to prove. My soul mate resolutely refused to discuss why she had left. Our alleged friends had made things worse. I couldn't take it anymore. Standing there on a city sidewalk, I broke down, a grown man sobbing in public. I remember the cheerful voices of a couple of little Pakistani kids chirping from a window somewhere above me; I remember turning away from traffic so no one would see my face.

I could have melted into a puddle of self-pity, but instead something interesting happened. Like many artists struggling to make it in the city, I had often focused on my own problems to the detriment of my concern for others. Now, on the way to meet brokers, I sat on the subway, staring across the aisle at the other riders. I no longer scoffed at bad haircuts or silly outfits; I saw sad, distracted people and I recognized that they were just like me.

Soon after that sad day, my apartment search reached an ugly climax. I was in a broker's office filling out an application when a big man walked in. He raised his voice, and then shoved the broker against a back wall. At first I thought he was just horsing around, but he began to shout into the man's face. And then—and this was the only time I have ever seen such a thing—he began to punch holes through the wall. Four of them, big ones, circling the broker's frightened face.

I dashed out to a store next door. "You have to call nine-one-one! Someone's about to get killed!"

Cautiously, I went back and peered into the broker's office. He was alive, thankfully, and the big man was gone.

"What happened?" I asked. "Was that guy crazy or what?"

The broker shook his head. "He was drunk. He was looking for his ex-wife, who used to work here."

I stumbled back out into the heat; this was too much to deal with after a long brutal day. I started thinking about the big man's rage against a woman he had once loved. I thought about his anger, and I thought about my own.

an empty cup

Shortly before Claire left, when we were in the midst of our troubles, I was on my way out of a coffee shop near Washington Square Park when I noticed a small sign on a bulletin board: *How to Deal With Anger*.

I stopped to read the rest; it advertised a Buddhist talk to be given in a yoga studio in Park Slope, Brooklyn. The location alone gave me doubts. Park Slope is notorious as one of the city's premier bastions of baby-boomer New Agers. I lived in Washington, D.C., during the great peace marches of the sixties. My family was pretty liberal, and we had college students from all over the country camp out in our living room so they could join in, and we all listened to Joan Baez sing at the base of the Washington Monument. I witnessed the great spirit of hope of those years, but also their dopey, naïve side.

As for the Buddhist part, I didn't know much about it. What I *thought* I knew came from a mishmash of media images. As a kid, I had been awed and frightened by newsreels of Buddhist monks in orange robes setting fire to themselves to protest the Vietnam War. More recently, I had read gossip columns about Richard Gere and the Beastie Boys performing at concerts for a free Tibet.

What ideas did I pick up about Buddhism along the way?

That it was foreign.

That there was something New Agey about it.

That it involved mystical mumbo-jumbo.

That it was like a cult.

That it required a fanatical level of devotion.

Or that it was a fad, an affectation for celebrities.

Like many Westerners, I was ready to write the whole thing off. I could have just walked on past that sign, but something gave me pause. Maybe it was the calm authority of the title.

How to Deal with Anger.

Not *An Attempt to Understand Anger.*

Not *How to Get Blissed-Out and Pretend You're Not Really Angry.*

The first part of the title offered a direct promise. A "how-to" is a practical guide; it offers a method. To do what? Not to rationalize, to repress, or to deny. Like many Westerners, I imagined that Buddhism involved becoming so indifferent that you didn't have to worry about life's problems. This title pledged something else: that I could learn to *deal with* anger. And the last word was also direct and uncompromising. This would not be a talk about *miscommunication,* or *conflict,* or *disagreement.* No, it would concern *anger.* Such a raw, powerful word.

The talk promised answers. One reason why that struck me was that my wife and I were both, individually, seeing therapists at that time. There was no way in hell that they were ever going to come out and say: *Here's your problem. Here's what you can do about it.* I'm not knocking therapy, necessarily—and I'll talk more about this later—but the two methods of dealing with problems seemed radically different. Therapists—at least ones who come out of a Freudian tradition—are not supposed to tell you what's wrong with you, and they're certainly not supposed to tell you how to fix it.

Yet here was a sign for a talk that purported to do both. In two hours.

It seemed preposterous.

But I knew that I was having problems, and therapy didn't seem to be giving me the tools to deal with them.

What did I have to lose?

Ten bucks, and two hours of my time.

◖

The talk didn't conform to any of my prejudices or expectations.

I arrived early at the yoga studio. A young woman at the front desk asked me to remove my shoes, and I was glad that I had worn a relatively new pair of socks. She directed me to a plain, bare room with a polished wood floor, where I found several rows of chairs. That was a relief: my legs are not limber enough to pretzel into lotus position, and I doubted that my lower back would tolerate a couple of hours of sitting on the floor. I glanced at the other attendees as they arrived; there was not a single tie-dyed shirt in sight. They wore normal street clothes—in fact, they looked like a cross-section of people you might find on an average Midtown street. They nodded politely at me and at each other, then sat to await the teacher. The only clue that we might not be assembled for a night class on Screenwriting 101 or Managing Your Personal Finances was a colorful picture of the Buddha hanging above a chair at the front of the room.

The teacher arrived, another surprise. He wore Western clothes just like everybody else, and he was not a wizened little Asian man. He was Caucasian, younger than me, and he greeted us with a small calm smile. His name was Matthew.

He sat in his chair, facing us, and set down a bottle of water and a book. "We'll start, as always, with a short period of meditation. Please sit up straight, with your feet resting comfortably on the floor. You can put your hands on your knees or in your lap, or you can turn them up and rest your right hand on your left, with your thumbs touching like this. Now close your eyes." He spent a couple of minutes directing us to relax each part of our bodies, from the crown of our heads on down to our toes.

I played along. It couldn't hurt to relax a little, right?

"Now let's concentrate on our breathing. Pay attention to the sensation at the front of your nostrils as the air comes in and the air goes out. Try to forget about everything else—all of your thoughts and worries of the day—and just focus on your breathing."

Eyes closed, we sat in silence. I tried to think about nothing but my breath, but soon realized that I was thinking about *everything* else. The teacher seemed young—would he have the authority to teach me anything worthwhile? The woman two seats to my left had looked pretty sexy. A car horn bleated annoyingly outside the studio. My stomach gurgled—did anyone else hear it? I thought of a yoga class a friend had talked me into a couple of years before—it was surprisingly strenuous, and there was a moment when I worried that my back might snap, and we ended with a period of meditation where we lay on the mats and closed our eyes, and then I heard some strange wordless moaning and a familiar voice droning "They swam in the ancient oceans" and I barely restrained myself from bursting out in laughter as I realized that it was a tape of Leonard "Spock" Nimoy reciting a poem over songs of humpback whales. . . .

"Stay focused on your breath." Matthew's calm voice pulled me back into the present and I realized how far my mind had strayed from that simplest of tasks.

Hmm, I thought. *This is not as easy as it sounds.*

After about twenty minutes, Matthew brought the meditation to a close. I felt pleasantly relaxed, but that was all. I certainly had not received any mind-expanding insights.

Matthew began his talk. I sat back with my ingrained skepticism. *I'll give this a shot, but the minute I hear any whale songs, I'm out of here.* I wasn't looking forward to any chanting or rituals either.

My birth religion was Judaism. When I was a kid, for a couple of years I was sent to Hebrew school a couple of afternoons a week. I was never attracted by the pomp and ritual. I didn't understand why I should practice a certain religion simply because I had been born into it. I had to memorize prayers in a language I didn't even know. I was something of a dissident, the kid who was never content to receive instruction without asking *Why?* One afternoon, my younger brother and I rebelled completely: when it came time to head off to the classes, we climbed a tree and hid.

(I would soon discover that many of the Westerners attracted to Buddhism have been Jewish. Maybe part of the reason is the fact that Buddhists make a clear distinction between *remorse,* which can be useful, and *guilt,* which is not.)

◙

I had never practiced an Eastern religion before, but I did have some exposure to Chinese martial arts. I briefly studied Shaolin kung fu—I guess those childhood years of watching the TV show left me with a secret desire to learn a few high kicks myself—and for four years I practiced tai chi. By the end of those years, I was helping my teacher train new students. I noticed that some were very open and eager to learn, while others were stubborn and resistant. During that time, I came across a helpful story about a Zen master. When confronted with a cocky student who acted like he already knew it all, he invited the young man to join him for tea. When the student sat down, the master set a cup in front of him and filled it up. He didn't stop, though: he kept pouring until the tea flowed down the sides of the cup—and he kept pouring. The student watched in surprise until the tea splashed onto the floor.

"Master," he cried. "What are you doing? You can't pour tea into a full cup!"

"Precisely," the master replied, and showed him out.

Like the student in the story, I was full of opinions and ideas about how life worked, including something of a chip on my shoulder about organized religion. Under normal circumstances, I might well have closed my mind to Matthew's talk.

In this sense, though, I think that Claire's stubborn refusal to speak with me did me a favor. If she had told me that she was having an affair or given some other simple reason for her departure, I would have been hurt, but would likely have clung to my old ideas. Instead, I was shaky and uncertain—I had more room than usual in my cup. I imagine it must be like that when a loved one dies: they leave a silence we yearn to fill.

Despite my qualms, it soon became apparent that this talk would not center on rote learning or blind faith. Matthew continually invited the class to challenge what he was saying. "You need to keep asking yourself, *Does this make sense in the light of my own experience?*" There was no chanting, no ceremony, no foreign languages, no memorization. He just talked, using plain English, full of anecdotes about everyday life, laced with humor. The notion that most of his ideas originated with ancient Indian and Tibetan monks still seemed a bit bizarre, but the talk was surprisingly practical and worldly. Matthew talked about how we see a pretty or handsome person on the street and feel an immediate intense attraction, or joked about annoying car alarms. He discussed how to deal with an oppressive boss, a difficult friendship, a love affair gone bad. There was little of religion's pomp and supernaturalism, and none of psychotherapy's reluctance to be direct.

Matthew said that Buddhists take anger very seriously. He noted how it leads to so many problems in the world: abuse, divorce, murder, war. He explained that it sows many seeds of future suffering, and briefly mentioned the concept of karma. That word sent up a little red flag for me. I had always felt that religion developed as a reaction to our fear of the unknown. It offered a comforting sense that everything happens for a reason, but I didn't believe that.

In any case, I wasn't there to debate metaphysics. I just wanted to reduce my anger.

What could the solution be?

I expected Matthew to offer ways to calm down, to chill out, to suppress. Maybe meditation was like a tranquilizing pill.

Instead, he pointed us in a completely unexpected direction.

does this book exist?

Midway through his talk, Matthew picked up the paperback he had set down at the beginning. He asked, "How many of you believe that this book has an independent existence outside of your mind?"

What? We were hesitant, suspicious of a trick, but most of us raised our hands.

"How do you know that it exists?"

Answers bounced back. "I can touch it." "If I drop it, I can hear it fall."

"So you know the book exists because your senses tell your mind that it exists?"

A bit reluctantly, we nodded.

"Is there any other way you know that this book exists?"

We struggled with that question for a few minutes, only to give up. Nothing we came up with—things we had been taught about books, things we had heard about books, books we had personally read—fell outside that fundamental category.

I grew wary. Was he saying that the book *didn't* exist? That it was only an illusion in our minds? That everything in the world was only an illusion? As a writer, one category of art has always bugged me. In its simplest form, it uses a trick ending: *And then I woke up and discovered that it had all been just a dream.* In a subtler and supposedly more adult form, it asks, *What is real and what is illusion, and how can we really know the difference?* The result is a lot of pretentious nonsense that poses as "avant-garde." (Most of us know full well that we don't have the luxury of musing whether the rent or utility bills *really* must be paid.)

I was worried that Matthew was heading off into that swampy territory. As it turned out, though, his aim was altogether different. For the purpose of this particular talk, he was not asking us to question whether the book truly existed. The point—and it turned out to be a monumental one—was that literally everything we feel and "know" about life is filtered through our own senses and our minds.

He began to point out some very big implications. "There are many things we can't change about the world, but we *can* change the way our mind perceives and reacts to them. Our sadness and happiness and anger don't have some independent reality outside of us—they come only from *within*." He smiled. "This is great news. It means that we have the potential to master our emotions, rather than letting them rule us."

In Matthew's typical style, he gave a concrete example, one that remains my favorite illustration of Buddhist principles. "Say you're on the subway," he began. "Now imagine that someone sits down next to you, and they're doing something you find very annoying. Maybe they're singing along with their iPod, or talking loudly, or popping their gum. Our typical way to think of this situation is, *Oh no, an external problem has just intruded into my life.* I could try to do something about it, maybe by telling the person to shut up or to go away, but this is the New York subway—if I do that, I might end up in a fight, or even get hurt or killed. So I'm going to sit here fuming, thinking *This problem irritates me. I have no choice but to get angry.*"

I could empathize all too well. I had always gotten annoyed when someone popped their gum in public, or blathered into a cell phone. I nearly got beat up once when I asked a young urban gangster and his pals to keep it down during a screening of *Gangs of New York.*

Matthew continued. "How could we deal with this situation differently? How about this? What if we were working really hard on developing patience? When that person sat down next to us, we could say, *Great! I'm trying to develop patience, and here comes a perfect opportunity to practice.* All of a sudden, the 'problem' isn't a problem anymore.

"Notice what happened here: *the external situation didn't change in any way. That person is still doing the exact same thing that bugged you before. The only thing that changed was your mind.* The problem wasn't 'out there' after all. In fact, the only place it existed was inside your head."

I was intrigued. I had come to a Buddhist talk on how to deal with anger, expecting advice about how to bliss out. I was expecting a talk about *feelings.* Instead, Matthew was offering a new way of *thinking* about life. That anecdote about the subway might seem trivial, but it slowly began to open up for me, like a small flower that blooms larger and larger, or one of those tiny dinosaurs that you buy at a science museum—put it in water and it grows. Years later, it continues to expand. (Eventually, I would discover that the subway story contains the seeds of the hardest to understand but most profound Buddhist teaching of all.)

Okay, you may be saying at this point, *I can see how this little story might help you deal with someone popping their gum, but surely it doesn't apply to bigger problems, like the death of a family member, or when a marriage breaks up.*

Here's a question, though: *Why not?*

If this idea can help with a little problem, why can't it help with the big ones?

One of my beefs in our marriage was that my wife continually took on new freelance responsibilities, often unpaid ones—and then she would complain about how much work she had to do, as if all of those chores had somehow been imposed on her by the universe. She seemed unable to see that her hectic, harried lifestyle was something she had created for herself. I was irritated by her view that all her problems were coming from outside, but now I had to wonder if I wasn't doing the same thing. Wasn't I saying, She's *making me angry,* as if I had no choice in the matter?

Matthew argued clearly that I did. In the West we have a strong sense that thought and feeling are very different things, and we even speak of them as originating in separate parts of the body (the head and the heart). The idea that I could use my mind to gain control over my emotions—to choose not to get angry, say, or learn not to be unhappy— seemed alien and odd. If Matthew was right, though, my anger was coming—not from some fuzzy feeling in my heart—but from a mistaken way of thinking about the world.

In fact, this Buddhism didn't seem like a traditional religion at all, but more of a practical psychology.

"In the West," Matthew continued, "we've spent thousands of years becoming very technologically advanced. We have our cars, our space shuttles, our computers, our bombs. We have developed countless ways to manipulate our external situation. For twenty-five hundred years, though, Buddhists have spent their time and energy exploring their *internal* world."

I realized that he was not offering some quick, easy insight that could suddenly wipe out all my pain. I couldn't just say, *Oh, my problems are all in my head,* and expect them to magically disappear. But what if I could gradually train my mind so that I wouldn't go around seeing "external problems" every-where? What if I could learn how to avoid anger altogether?

From that very first talk, I got an inkling that such things might be possible. Not just for highly trained monks in remote Himalayan caves, but for *anybody.*

Including me.

Including you.

In light of that talk, something really clicked for me several months later when I saw the man punching holes around the real estate agent. I realized that his anger was not some in-evitable, necessary reaction to external problems. It was all coming out of his own head. And his violence was certainly not proving anything to his wife; the only person he was punishing was himself. (Literally—when the alcohol wore off he would discover that the cops were looking for him, and that he had given himself a broken hand.)

I realized that I had been walking through the streets of Brooklyn carrying an unnecessary weight. The heat was bad enough, and the apartment search was worse; what good was it doing to add the burden of my anger? I resolved to try to set it down. I was so resentful about my wife's abandonment that I had warned her to stay away from our home until I found a new place. The next day, though, I called her up, doing my best to keep a civil tone, and invited her to come by and do whatever she needed to prepare for her own move. She did, and I was surprised at how calm I managed to be.

I was proud of myself, but—more importantly—I was impressed with the Buddhist teachings. They were not pie-in-the-sky abstractions, but practical instructions. They were not just about how to think better, but how to *behave* better. And life—especially in the crucible of a divorce—is really a continual series of decisions about how to act. Am I going to remain calm, or react in anger? Am I going to act out of a wounded sense of self, or out of compassion for someone else?

As Matthew had suggested, I had put his Buddhist insights to the test—and they seemed to work.

Of course, like most resolutions, my decision to avoid anger was subject to slip. And I was still walking around with a bitter diatribe running non-stop in my head. I fantasized about nasty things I could say to Claire to make her hurt the way I was hurting. And I fantasized about hurtful things I could say to our mutual friends who had abandoned ship. I could almost taste the satisfaction of these imagined acts of revenge. I even wished I could light into Claire's therapist: *Is this what you tell your patients, that it's acceptable for a mature adult to walk out on a marriage without a word of explanation??*

I needed to constantly remind myself that expressing anger could only bring bad results. A few days later, I would be presented with far more drastic evidence of that fact.

if anger wins

After I left the broker's office I was in a daze. The scene I had just witnessed seemed like the culmination of a nightmare. I desperately needed some good news.

As I trudged off down the block, I noticed an untraditional-looking real estate office, a rumpled little storefront with dusty houseplants in the window and a couple of comfy sofas replacing the usual drab office furniture. The broker was a tiny curly-haired woman with a spirited posture. A bearded bear of a man sat on one couch, and a pretty red-haired woman occupied the other. They greeted me with smiles.

I explained my situation to the broker and she nodded thoughtfully. "I have just the thing for you." She turned to the others. "Would you like to take a ride?"

The bearded man turned out to be her husband. The young woman was a client who had become a pal. I felt as if I had escaped a brutal action movie and wandered into an Ann Tyler novel, a cozy world inhabited by friendly, quirky characters. We all piled into the broker's cluttered little car and off we went, around Prospect Park and into another world. I was familiar with the elegant brownstones of Park Slope and the drab apartment buildings and bodegas that cover so much of the rest of Brooklyn, but we entered a neighborhood that seemed like it belonged somewhere altogether different, a picturesque old Southern town, with big Victorian houses with front porches overlooking tree-lined streets. After we pulled up in front of one of those houses, the broker showed me an apartment with some stained glass windows, a chandelier in the dining room, a big back patio, and much more room than my old place. The rent was higher than I had been paying, yet very reasonable by New York standards. I could hardly believe it; things were finally looking up. Not only was I not homeless, but I could even end up with a nicer place than my old apartment. "I'll take it," I said, incredibly relieved. My new friends and I went to a nearby Mexican restaurant to celebrate.

The broker told me that the owner lived out of town. I couldn't seem to pin down where, exactly, but didn't let that bother me. (Don't look a gift horse in the mouth.) I got the keys a few days early so I could stop by and clean the place up.

On my way up to the porch, I was hailed by a neighbor. I explained that I was moving in, and asked if she knew anything about the owner of the house. She gave me an odd look.

"You mean you don't know?"

I gave her a puzzled look back. "Don't know what? I was told he lives out of town."

She sighed. "He does. He's in prison."

My chest went heavy. "He is? What for?"

She made a pained face. "He killed his wife."

My chest got heavier, and I asked another question, even though I already sensed the answer. "He killed her *where?*"

In my new apartment.

The neighbor gave me the gist of the story. The landlord was not some obvious criminal type; he was a respectable family man with a steady job and two kids. He and his wife were going through a rough time, but the neighbors hardly ever heard them raise their voices. One night, apparently, they were having an argument and something inside him snapped.

I sagged back and raised a feeble hand. I didn't want to know the details, except where it had happened (the bathroom). I groaned. What was I going to do? I had already paid the broker and the first month's rent. I had only a few days to vacate my old place.

Under other circumstances I might still have fled, but when I thought about starting over with my apartment hunt, about trudging back into that wilderness of absurd rents and nutty roommates, of shifty brokers and unmerciful co-op boards, I couldn't face it. This was merely the capper on the worst summer of my life. I called my broker, who seemed genuinely ignorant of the tragic story, and told her that I planned to stay.

I was terribly sorry to hear about the murder in my new apartment. I was sorry for the victim, of course, and sorry for the kids, whose lives would be forever scarred. I was also sorry for the killer, a man swamped by anger, who in one stark moment suddenly wrecked four lives, including his own.

I moved in. The first week, I definitely felt weird, even when I wasn't thinking about the murder. After I turned off all the lights at night, it was strange enough to be in bed alone, without my wife. Strange to be in a completely different bedroom, after sixteen years. On top of all that, I tried not to picture what might have happened in my new bathroom. One night I heard an odd clanking sound that seemed to be coming from that region, and I imagined that it was the anguished ghost of the former lady of the house—until I realized that it was just the basement furnace heating up.

I soon adjusted. I know that a dark thing happened in the house, but I'm not superstitious. I think about the woman who once lived here. I don't believe in an afterlife, but if there is one, I wish her well. I try to fill the place with a positive attitude, a determination to be more compassionate and kind.

Above all, the terrible thing that happened in my apartment serves as a daily reminder and inspiration: *This is what can happen if you let anger win.*

one for the seesaw

I have read novels in which a character's spouse goes out for a pack of cigarettes and spontaneously decides to keep on walking, but I doubt that happens much in real life. I imagine that Claire must have spent considerable time working herself up to leave our marriage. When she did, it came as little surprise to her.

I wish I could say the same.

Marriage makes me think of a seesaw: you have your ups and your downs, but through them all you trust your partner to support your weight. If one spouse suddenly jumps off, the other comes down hard. The whole solemn institution, which seemed so solid and permanent — *We'll love each other for better or for worse, until we die* — is revealed as merely a fragile, tenuous, utterly voluntary agreement.

And one partner can simply take it back.

After Claire jumped away, my tailbone ached and so did my heart, but — like someone embarrassed to have fallen in public—I did my best to put on a stoic front. *You don't need her,* I told myself. *In fact, you're better off without her.* I reminded myself of Nietzsche's old chestnut: *What doesn't kill us makes us stronger.* Some days, propped up with self-righteous anger, I even managed to feel strong.

Then night would fall.

I would dream that I was desperately searching for my wife. After terrible dark struggles, I'd find her and wrap my arms around her, weeping with relief and joy, bursting with all the love I had ever felt for her. And then she would push me away, or disappear, and I'd just plain weep, and wake up, and the goddamned pillow would be wet.

The fact that some of our mutual friends had abruptly stopped talking to me amplified the pain unbearably. One— this blew my mind—actually said that she had only so much sympathy to give, and she had decided to offer it to Claire. I could have understood that if I had cheated on my wife, or if I was the one who had bailed out. But no—we were just two adults with conflicting approaches to life. I couldn't understand why our friends felt that they needed to take sides. (Naïve, I know—I'll come back to this later on.)

I felt a crushing sense of isolation, relieved by a few kind friends who stepped up and watched out for me; they invited me to dinner on the lonely weekends, called to see how I was holding up. I owe them more than I can say.

◁

I also found relief by going to more Buddhist talks. I discovered that each one focused on a specific, very practical topic: How to Develop Harmonious Relationships, or How to Deal With Jealousy, or How to Calm the Mind. I was intrigued by what I was hearing, but had my doubts. The whole thing still seemed foreign, and sometimes I wondered if I was not just reaching out in desperation to some fad or cult.

But I began to notice something: I never felt bad while I was listening to a talk, and I'd feel better for hours or days afterward.

It wasn't just the message that buoyed me. In those isolated days, I was glad to have somewhere to go where I could be with other people, some of whom were also going through hard times. I started becoming friends with Jane, a quiet real estate broker and single mother who had gone through her own divorce years before. And Barbara, a lively commercial sign designer, struggling with the ups and downs of her current relationship with her girlfriend. These were people I might not have met before my marriage ended, when I tended to seek out friends of my same age or career or interests. I had never been much of a joiner. I believed in self-sufficiency, in my power to solve my own problems. That solidarity can offer profound comfort will not be news to anyone who is a member of AA, or a church fellowship, or even an association of hobbyists, but to me it came as a pleasant discovery.

I was also surprised by the humor that laced the teachings. There was no sanctimony. I started going to Buddhist talks at various places around the city, including a Unitarian church in Brooklyn Heights. Those were given by a woman named Gen-la Dekyong, who—despite the Tibetan name— was an Irish Buddhist nun. She spoke with an incredibly soothing, quiet voice, and she laughed all the time—at her own foibles, at ours, at things that happened which she couldn't control. Once when she was giving a talk, a choral group began practicing in the rec room next door. Instead of asking them to keep it down—or exhibiting any frustration or anger—she simply accepted that she had competition. As she went on, she would be working up to some profound point when the singers would burst in with a heavenly chorus. She began to smile, and then to laugh outright at this accidental soundtrack. Her talks often concerned the most serious of subjects—like dealing with fear or doubt or the prospect of death—but her sense of lightness, her willingness to see the humor in things, seemed ever present.

That provided a very important example for me, because I was still walking around playing an angry tape loop in my head.

Luckily, because I was learning more about anger, most of the time I managed to avoid acting on my bitter fantasies of revenge. I discovered that my anger arose when life didn't give me something I wanted, or when it presented me with something I *didn't* want.

I still got angry, though. I remember one time when I was waiting in a long line at the post office. A man walked in, sussed out the situation, and ducked into the line ahead of me. Immediately, I felt that red heat flare up inside me. How did this jerk think he could get away with such rude behavior? How dare he think that he was better than anybody else! I wanted to spin him around and chew him out in front of the whole crowd. I didn't say anything, though—I just stood there and fumed. And then—because of the Buddhist talks—I was able to notice how upset I had gotten over such a trivial thing.

By the way, you may notice that I talk about anger a lot. There are two reasons for this. First, it's the most obviously destructive emotion in a marriage. Second, it was a big part of my own experience of divorce. Your troubles may feel different: maybe you get depressed rather than angry, turning your unhappiness inward. Maybe your main emotion is remorse, or guilt about the way your relationship ended. If you think about it, though, all these feelings have something essential in common: they arise out of dissatisfaction with the way life turned out, and disappointment that the world is not the way we want it to be. Luckily, they have something else in common: they originate solely in our minds.

And because I was starting to pay attention to what was going on in my mind, I made an essential discovery: my anger almost always bloomed out of an inner sense of hurt. That hurt seemed intolerable, so I would try to get rid of it by projecting it outside. In the long run, such relief was illusory: anger *always* made things worse.

If I could learn to recognize the roots of my anger, though, maybe I could learn to put a little gap between the match and the "inevitable" flare-up. In that small, vital breathing space, I might discover that I had more than one way to react. I was beginning to learn that this was one of the major reasons to meditate. It wasn't about blissing out; it was about becoming *more* aware of the way my mind worked. Buddhists call this awareness *mindfulness,* and consider it the foundation for their whole spiritual practice. (The *Buddha,* after all, means "The Awakened One.")

As I discovered during my very first meditation session with Matthew, gaining a serene mastery of the mind is a hell of a task. Zen Buddhists refer to our normal uncontrolled thought process as *monkey mind,* and it's easy to see why: we swing wildly from branch to branch, grasping at appealing objects, skittering away from unpleasant ones. We don't feel we have much choice about where the monkey leaps next.

Buddhism promised that this wild creature could be tamed.

⟡

So, you may well ask, *why didn't I use all of this new knowledge to save my marriage?* The answer is simple: there's a big distance between gaining an intellectual understanding and being able to put it to use. I tried in small ways, but—like a musician who has just picked up a new instrument—I simply didn't have sufficient skill. If I had encountered Buddhism a year earlier, perhaps I would still be married today.

Or not.

Who knows?

if drinkin' don't kill me

had suffered through some bad breakups in the past, and it had taken me a long time to get over some of them. I remember wallowing in misery because I didn't know that I had any other option.

This time, if I hadn't stumbled across Buddhism, I'm sure I would have followed the same downward trajectory. I might have tried to dull the pain. I probably would have drunk more alcohol than usual. I might have been unable to eat for a while, but then I might have eaten too much. I might have sought out casual sex in a hopeless attempt to blot out memories of making love with Claire. If I had more money, I might have gone out and bought things to try to fill the hole she left in my life. None of those diversions would have truly relieved my suffering.

Not even country music.

While the blues expresses an overall existential sadness, country pins it on one notorious cause: *My baby left.* And no one sings that heartbreak better than George Jones. In song after song, in a powerful, yearning voice that always makes me think of whiskey laced with honey, he strings together one primordial tale of woe. The narrator's wife leaves him, without explanation. As she goes, he hears the most terrible sound in the world, "the closing of the door." He suffers crushing grief, a sense that his world has been stripped to nothing.

I love George Jones, and listening to such songs gave me the sense that I wasn't alone in my despair. I listened to Johnny Cash too—one song in particular. I'd put on my headphones, and go for a run in nearby Prospect Park, out in the chilly fall afternoons, with dead leaves falling all around me, as Johnny's deep voice boomed out, "Oh, no, I never got over those blue eyes/ I see them everywhere/ I miss those arms that held me/ When all the love was there/ I wonder if she's sorry/ For leavin' what we'd begun . . . "

I didn't lack for songs of ruined love—my iPod was full of them. Gradually, though, I started to notice something: they seemed to put a salve on the pain, but shared one huge shortcoming. They didn't offer any real way out.

For the first time, something pretty obvious occurred to me: the sad songs were just helping me stay sad.

There's a lot of talk floating around these days about how we have to accept our emotions and process them before we can move on. That's true, up to a point. Beyond that point, though, we risk deepening the power of those feelings. For example, some therapists encourage punching a pillow to work through anger. Considering new studies in neuroscience, that doesn't seem like a very good idea. Researchers have found that such behavior actually increases aggression; expressing anger in this way helps to build and strengthen the neural pathways for that unpleasant emotion—the last thing we want to do. And from a Buddhist standpoint, expressing anger is never a helpful thing to do. The idea is certainly not to deny or repress anger or sadness or other painful feelings. The goal is to acknowledge them, gain the insight to see how they arose, understand that they don't have to control us, and then let them go. Buddhism offers very specific ways to work toward that.

As it happened, I didn't become one of George Jones's barroom drunks. I was beginning to sense that maybe—just maybe—I might have found an alternative. The small number of talks I had attended were enough to convince me that this new spiritual realm might have more to offer than just some intriguing concepts. My interest in an end to suffering was not at all abstract.

If such a thing was possible, I wanted it—*bad*.

⌐

And then, several months after my first Buddhist talk, I stumbled upon one thin paperback.

There are certain books that people pass on to each other in times of crisis. Get cancer and a friend might give you *Love, Medicine and Miracles*. Lose a child and someone will likely offer Harold S. Kushner's *When Bad Things Happen to Good People*. In the Western Buddhist world, and—increasingly—outside of it, the go-to book is called *When Things Fall Apart: Heart Advice for Difficult Times*.

I found it in an ironic way. Several months before Claire left, one of her best friends left her own husband and came to stay with us in our house's empty third-floor bedroom. When Claire and I split up, her friend moved out, but she left the book behind. I found myself alone in the empty house, wandering around aimlessly — "walking the floor over you," as the old country song put it — and I came across it one sweltering summer afternoon.

The author photo showed a woman in a Buddhist nun's red and orange robes. Her name was Pema Chödrön and she was a middle-aged Caucasian with close-cropped hair and a confident face that bore a slight suggestion of a smile. She reminded me of the regal British actress Judi Dench.

I lay down on the dusty bedspread and began to read. Quickly, I became impressed with Chödrön's frank, no-nonsense tone. "When the bottom falls out and we can't find anything to grasp, it hurts a lot. . . . We look in the bathroom mirror, and there we are with our pimples, our aging face, our lack of kindness, our aggression and timidity — all that stuff." As I read, every few minutes I would stop and turn to the author photo. Who was this woman? What set her on such an unusual path?

On page ten, I found out. It was not some vague yearning for spirituality, not some dry intellectual interest. My eyes widened. Before she became a nun, Chödrön and her husband were living in New Mexico. (Her *husband* — that was a surprise in itself.) "I was standing in front of our adobe house," she wrote. "I heard the car drive up and the door bang shut. Then he walked around the corner, and without warning he told me that he was having an affair and wanted a divorce. I remember the sky and how huge it was. I remember the sound of the river and the steam rising up from my tea. There was no time, no thought, there was nothing — just the light and a profound, limitless stillness. Then I regrouped and picked up a stone and threw it at him."

I was riveted. This was not some tale from thousands of years ago, not some foreign monk preaching esoteric texts. I felt an instant kinship with this stranger in her colored robes, this woman abandoned by her spouse.

The next paragraph surprised me. "When anyone asks me how I got involved in Buddhism, I always say it was because I was so angry with my husband. The truth is that he saved my life. When that marriage fell apart, I tried hard—very, very hard—to go back to some kind of comfort, some kind of security, some kind of familiar resting place."

I could certainly relate to that feeling of groundlessness. To use the old cliché, Claire had yanked the rug out from under me, and I felt shaky and uneasy. As it became clear that she was gone for good, I realized that I had lost more than my bond with her in the present. My future had disappeared as well. It had taken me a long time to reach a point where I felt ready for married life, and I was just starting to come to terms with the idea of becoming a father. Now the family I'd been envisioning had vaporized in one stark instant.

I thought of that Valentine's Day present I had given to Claire, the one with a picture of two rocking chairs side by side.

Suddenly I was rocking into a completely uncertain future. Alone.

When things fall apart, indeed.

I read on, wondering how Pema Chödrön succeeded in returning to firmer ground.

"Fortunately for me," she writes, "I could never pull it off. Instinctively I knew that annihilation of my old dependent, clinging self was the only way to go."

Annihilation of self? That didn't sound so great, but Chödrön's direct, honest voice made me trust her. She went on to explain how she discovered—through Buddhism—that her profound feeling of groundlessness was okay; that it wasn't something that needed to be fixed.

I was surprised again, a reaction that would become routine as I became more familiar with Buddhism. Its teachings often run counter to conventional wisdom. One story expresses this literally. Talking about fear, Chödrön recounts a tale told by her teacher, a Tibetan lama named Chögyam Trungpa Rinpoche. Once, when he traveled to a strange monastery with his attendants, a snarling guard dog broke free and rushed at them. The attendants screamed and fled, but Trungpa ran right toward the dog, which was so astonished that it turned tail and ran.

Trungpa offered the same remarkable advice about suffering. While we try so hard to run away from it or deny it, he advised "leaning into the sharp points." Stay with the pain. Feel it fully. The result, Chödrön said, could be the opposite of what we expect. We panic when we're not in control, but we can learn to accept our lack of power over everything. We can let our fear go. Instead of searching desperately for firmer ground, we may discover that uncertainty and not-knowing are okay. "To stay with that shakiness," writes Chödrön, "to stay with a broken heart, a rumbling stomach, with the feeling of hopelessness and wanting to get revenge—that is the path of true awakening. Sticking with that uncertainty, getting the knack of relaxing in the midst of chaos, learning not to panic—this is the spiritual path."

What a relief! I was in a bitter cycle: feeling depressed, feeling angry and lost, feeling depressed that I was angry. But maybe that was all right. Maybe I didn't have to feel bad about my "bad" emotions. *Stop beating yourself up*, this woman was saying. Be more open, less frightened of uncertainty and change. *Be kinder to yourself, and you'll open up to the whole world.*

Through the murk of my suffering, I sensed—so unexpectedly!—that my calamity was beginning to take on the outlines of an adventure.

what is buddhism?

Before I go on discussing my encounters with "Buddhism," I think I should acknowledge that the term is a bit vague. It's like saying that I discovered *Christianity:* I could be talking about a world of white-gloved Park Avenue Episcopalians, or a world of snake-handling backwoods tent-revivalists. I wouldn't say that the range of Buddhist practice is quite that extreme, but as I started exploring it, I realized that I had entered a big river through just one of a number of different streams.

Matthew was teaching a particular tradition of Tibetan Buddhism. Those insights had flowed from a remote realm of snow-capped mountains to a yoga studio on the more modest incline of Park Slope, Brooklyn, and I soon learned that other Buddhist traditions had spread to the West from other far places, ranging from dense forests in Thailand to mist-shrouded valleys in China to tranquil Japanese temples. (In the West, we tend to view Buddhism as something exotic, yet

I have to wonder if it is really more alien than a number of supernaturally oriented religions that originated in the ancient deserts of the Middle East.)

At first, the choices seemed confusing. I put a lot of mileage on my library and credit cards as I sought out books from a number of different schools. I discovered that Western Buddhism has several major strains. These include *Zen,* which developed in China, Japan, and Korea, and focuses on finding ways to bypass our busy conceptual minds in favor of more direct, immediate experience of the world. There's Tibetan *Mahayana* Buddhism, which seems a bit more like a traditional religion and focuses on learning how to attain enlightenment so that you can go on to help other people. And there's a more secular approach called *Vipassana,* or "insight meditation," which is based on Indian traditions, and centers on techniques for training the mind.

Though some teachers recommend studying one school exclusively, I decided early on that I would cast a wide net, fishing for helpful information wherever it might be found. The variety seemed a bit confusing, until I discovered that all of the streams trace their origin to the same geographical source (northern India), the same historical moment (five centuries before the start of the Christian era), and the same person, who started out as a prince named Siddhartha Gautama, and ended up as a sage known as the Buddha.

From the start, Buddhism was different from other religions. For one thing, as Jean Smith points out in her excellent *A Beginner's Guide to Zen Buddhism,* the Buddha was "the only founder of a major religion who claimed to be neither a god or a messenger of a god." In fact, Buddhism is not theistic — there's no notion of an omniscient or omnipotent god. What's more, the Buddha made no effort to say where the universe comes from. While other religions tried to explain natural phenomena—why it rained or didn't, why crops grew—and answer metaphysical questions—*Is there a heaven?*—he zeroed in on human problems and one essential, practical question: *How does the way we think about life shape our experience of it?* Mark Epstein, a psychiatrist who has written several fascinating books about common ground between Western therapy and Buddhism, calls it "the most psychological of religions, and the most spiritual of psychologies."

The person who came to be known as the Buddha made for an unusual spiritual leader. He didn't demand devotion or worship as a divinity—at first, he didn't even want to preach—and he certainly wasn't into threatening people if they didn't believe. He always said that he was just a human being, and that anyone could learn to do what he had done. As Jean Smith notes, he saw himself as a teacher, rather than a leader, and his ideas are referred to as "teachings," rather than rules or laws. Some consider him a religious figure, but we can also see him as a deeply interesting philosopher and a masterful psychologist.

In fact, I soon began to wonder whether "religion" is the right word for Buddhism at all. I came to prefer this description, offered by French Buddhist monk Matthieu Ricard in his book *Happiness: A Guide to Developing Life's Most Important Skill:* he calls it "a rich, pragmatic science of mind, an altruistic art of living, a meaningful philosophy, and a spiritual practice that [leads] to genuine inner transformation." Currently, there are an estimated three million practitioners of various schools of Buddhism in America, with many others who have been influenced by its ideas. They come to it for a number of reasons, ranging from stress reduction to spiritual awakening.

Because it doesn't offer a different deity and different cosmological beliefs, Buddhism doesn't necessarily clash with other religions. I discovered that you could be a follower of another faith—or even an atheist—and still adopt Buddhist practices and insights. (Albert Einstein once said that, "If there is any religion that would cope with modern scientific needs, it would be Buddhism.")

All of the traditions share a central core: they're founded on the teachings of the Buddha, which are known as the *Dharma,* and they use meditation as their central practice. Most of the insights we'll explore here are common to the various schools.

One of the absolutely central ideas is that becoming a Buddhist is not about adopting a rigid set of beliefs—it's about undertaking a personal journey and testing its ideas for yourself. Everybody's path is unique.

My next step started with a frozen turkey.

forgiveness

Despite Matthew's calming talks, and Pema Chödrön's excellent advice, I still felt lousy much of the time, and still wasn't doing a very good job of accepting the pain. I kept having sad dreams about Claire, and sleepless nights when I struggled, in vain, to come to grips with the baffling unkindness of some of our mutual friends. I had managed to set aside my anger long enough to be able to invite Claire back to get her things, but it often came charging back.

Maybe I've been glossing over the amount of resentment I really felt. I'm reminded of a joke about a chat between two psychoanalysts.

> One of them says, "The other day I made a classic Freudian slip. I was in Penn Station and the ticket seller was a very attractive young woman. I asked her for 'two pickets to Titsburgh.'"

"That's very funny," his colleague replies. "At breakfast this morning I did the same thing. I meant to ask my wife to pass the salt, but instead I said, 'You ruined my life, you bitch!'"

All too often, that's what I wanted to say—to shout—at Claire. *You've ruined everything!*

That bitter tape loop had some big problems.

First—and it took me a while to realize this remarkably obvious fact—all of the time and energy I was putting into my resentful diatribe wasn't going anywhere. My voice was just ricocheting around in my own head, turning it into a foolish echo chamber. It didn't affect Claire one bit. (To put it another way, I was punching holes in a wall she couldn't even see.)

Second, it didn't bring me any relief. When I blamed her, the loop just got louder and louder, and I made myself more agitated. (The fact that my wife firmly refused to talk didn't help. I pictured her therapist and girlfriends counseling her, *Don't engage with him. He'll just be angry.* Talk about a self-fulfilling prophecy . . .)

Fortunately, the Buddhist talks helped me see how destructive my anger could be. They helped me calm down somewhat, and I resolved to refrain from expressing any more anger toward Claire.

But it was still there. By that point—considering our minimal contact—it was probably hurting me more than it was her. I still carried a couple of grievances that I couldn't get over, and they were tearing me apart.

Even at that early stage, I somehow realized that I needed to take one positive action. I needed to do something radical, something that went against everything my anger was telling me to feel and do.

Before I could think about moving on, I needed to try and *forgive* her.

Two things helped me come to that understanding.

One of them was another book I stumbled across.

The other was a supermarket bird.

On November 13, 2004, a forty-four-year-old office manager named Victoria Ruvolo was driving along a highway on Long Island when her life changed in an instant. A car coming the other way contained a group of teenagers on a joy ride. One of them, eighteen years old, was holding a twenty-pound frozen turkey that they had just bought with a stolen credit card. On the spur of the moment, he decided that it would be fun to hurl it out at the approaching traffic. The object smashed through Ruvolo's windshield and hit her in the face. It caved in her esophagus, smashed both cheeks and her jaw, fractured one of her eye sockets, and damaged her brain. She survived the attack, but she was in critical condition when she was taken to the hospital.

On August 15, 2005, Victoria Ruvolo appeared at a court hearing for the youth who had so severely disrupted her life. He faced twenty-five years in prison if convicted, but Ruvolo asked the prosecutor to approve a very lenient plea bargain.

Here's what the *New York Times* reported about the scene:

> Stopping to speak to [Ruvolo] on his way out of the courtroom, [the defendant] choked on an apology and began to cry. For an intensely emotional few minutes, Ms. Ruvolo alternately embraced him tightly, stroked his face and patted his back as he sobbed uncontrollably.

Many of the two dozen people in court—prosecutors, court officers and reporters—choked back tears.

"I'm so sorry, so sorry," [the defendant] said over and over again. "I didn't mean it." Most of their exchange was inaudible, but at one point Ms. Ruvolo's advice to him was just barely audible.

"It's O.K., it's O.K.," she said. "I just want you to make your life the best it can be."

I read that story seven weeks after Claire left. The lawyers and court officers were not the only people to get choked up by Victoria Ruvolo's extraordinary kindness. I'm not going to even begin to claim that my situation was comparable to hers, but her story certainly made me reconsider how much of a grudge I was willing to carry.

❏

Around that same time, I was browsing in my local library when I came across a book by a man named Lewis B. Smedes. I had never heard of him before, but the title caught my attention: *Forgive and Forget: Healing the Hurts We Don't Deserve*. I quickly read that book and its sequel, *The Art of Forgiving: When You Need to Forgive and Don't Know How*.

Though Smedes was a Christian professor of theology and ethics, some of his ideas echo major elements of Buddhist thought. His message was not coated with any greeting card sugar. In his books, he recounted a number of stories of people who had been victimized even worse than Victoria Ruvolo. They included rape victims, victims of political torture, even Holocaust survivors. These people had spent years of their lives haunted by horrific memories. One after another, they had come to realize that there was only one way to free themselves from their traumatic pasts. You might think that the solution would be to get revenge, or at least to bring the perpetrators to justice, but even seeing their tormenters put behind bars often failed to bring them the release and relief they so desperately craved. As Smedes put it, "We sometimes get close to justice. We never bring closure to vengeance."

So what did they do to find real peace?

They *forgave* the ones who wronged them.

At first blush, this may seem strange. Unlike the teenager who hurled the turkey at Victoria Ruvolo, many of the perpetrators in Smedes's stories were not at all repentant. And many of them had not been brought to any kind of legal justice. So why forgive them? Wouldn't you have to be some kind of saint?

I had always thought that forgiveness was an act you did for someone else. As Smedes pointed out, though, it's largely something you can do to help yourself. If you can't do it, *you're* the one who has to carry the burden of your anger and other bad feelings. You don't even need to do it out loud. It is, above all, a deep transformation within your own heart. As Smedes so compellingly put it, "When we forgive, we set a prisoner free and discover that the person we set free is us."

He said that the first step is to "rediscover the humanity of the person who hurt us. [When we are wronged] we shrink him to the size of what he did. If he has done something truly horrible, we say things like, 'He is no more than an animal.' Or, 'He is nothing but a cheat.' Our 'no more thans' and our 'nothing buts' knock the humanity out of our enemy. . . . He is only, he is totally, the sinner who did us wrong." When we forgive, though, "We take him back into our private world as a person who shares our faulty humanity, bruised like us, faulty like us, still thoroughly blamable for what he did to us. Yet, human like us."

Even in those early days, I could see that my anger at Claire was causing me to see only her bad side; I was blocking out the four years of happiness we had shared, and all of the kind and loving things she had done. Forgiving didn't mean that I needed to excuse any wrongs she might have done. It meant that I could take a more compassionate, understanding view of why she did them—I could see that she had acted out of a desire to avoid pain, rather than any wish to hurt me.

As Smedes said, we don't forgive the person for who we think they are; we forgive them for the specific actions they have taken to wrong us. Buddhism puts that idea in a profound and surprising context: it says that a person's hurtful behavior does not reflect his or her essential nature *at all.* As the Tibetan spiritual leader Geshe Kelsang Gyatso puts it in his book *Transform Your Life: A Blissful Journey*:

> Living beings have no faults. . . . Although sentient beings' minds are filled with delusions, sentient beings themselves are not faulty. We say that sea water is salty, but in fact it is the salt in the water that makes it salty, not the water itself. [. . .] Similarly, all the faults we see in people are actually the faults of their delusions, not of the people themselves. . . . If someone is angry, we think 'He is a bad and angry person,' whereas Buddhas think 'He is a suffering being afflicted with the inner disease of anger.' If a friend of ours were suffering from cancer we would

not blame him for his physical disease, and, in the same way, if someone is suffering from anger or attachment we should not blame him for the diseases of his mind.

If someone hits us with a stick, Buddhists say, we should not waste time getting angry at the stick. Likewise, if someone wrongs us, we should not waste time being angry with the person—they're only being propelled by their delusions.

Seeing things in that bold light forced me to question the point of my resentment. And Smedes wrote so convincingly about the healing power of forgiveness that he made me want to try it with Claire—for both our sakes. I realized that the end of our marriage must have brought her considerable suffering too, especially if she was feeling any guilt for the way she had carried it out. Because I still loved her, I hoped to lift a small part of her burden.

As Smedes made clear, though, forgiveness is not about trying to get someone else to react in a certain way, which is lucky, because otherwise it would have failed dismally with Claire. I wrote to say that I forgave her for the way she had abandoned our marriage. She didn't acknowledge my note. I wrote again to say that I wished that her pain would soon give way to happiness, even if it had to be with someone else. Again, no response. I might as well have been dropping pennies into the Grand Canyon.

No matter. I still felt better.

In retrospect, I can see that I might have chosen an odd time to carry out this step in my divorce. True forgiveness is something that often takes years to reach, and in many stories it supplies the final chapter. It's not something you can manufacture or force; it can only come when you're ready for it. I don't know how deep my forgiveness really ran. But I *do* know that giving it a try enabled me drop some of my hostility; it opened a crack in my hardened heart. And it challenged me to start seeing my wife as a real person again, with complexities and sufferings of her own.

Ultimately, Claire would have to find herself a path out of the mess we had made.

All I could do was follow my own.

A man is taking an airplane flight cross-country. He notices that the woman next to him is wearing a huge, brilliant, and unusual diamond ring. He stares at it, and stares at it, and finally he speaks. "Excuse me, ma'am, I just have to say that I can't help looking at your amazing ring."

The woman smiles, rather sadly. "Yes, this is the famous Klopman Diamond. It's a beautiful gem, but unfortunately it comes with a curse."

The man is intrigued. "A curse? What is it?"

The woman shrugs. "Mr. Klopman."

σ

In divorce, it's tempting to pin the blame for our suffering on our partners. We think that if we can make them the villains, we'll somehow feel better about ourselves.

In my case, my wife certainly seemed to believe that the reason for her suffering was clear: *I* had thwarted her happiness; *I* was the cause of her pain. Just as she blamed her constant overwork and busyness on some cosmic external imposition, so she blamed the problems of our marriage on something outside of herself. The solution seemed simple: she got rid of the apparent source of her troubles.

I hope that worked for her.

The path of blame was tempting, but it couldn't work for me. I knew, in my heart of hearts, that it would be a cop-out. With my anger, my pride, my unwillingness to compromise, I had certainly shared in the destruction of our marriage.

When I was a kid, I wasn't very athletic, and I suffered from a mild case of acne, which damaged my self-esteem. I compensated in the only way I knew how: I did well academically. I could excel at one thing—and that was *being right*. That helped me get into a good college, and then it helped me get journalism work, but when I brought that particular talent into my marriage, the result was a disaster.

Before we got married, Claire and I went to a few sessions of couples therapy to make sure we'd be able to deal with some of our differences. The therapist encouraged us to think of ourselves as a "we," rather than just two separate individuals. She wisely suggested that we should always try to think about what was good for that *we*, and to put it before our own personal desires.

Somehow, though, in the heat of an argument I tended to lose sight of that sage counsel. I pressed my side with the tenacity of a trial lawyer. I can see now that this must have been very frustrating and dispiriting for Claire.

And what happened?

I won some battles.

I lost the war.

No, I couldn't just go around slinging blame. If there were any villains in the piece, one of them was me.

Even if we can put all the blame on our partner, that doesn't get us anywhere. Nowhere good, that's for sure. It only leads to more anger, more bitterness, more damage.

It points us down an ugly road. We might hire a lawyer who encourages us to think of our spouse as our enemy. If we have kids or joint property, it can get even nastier. Maybe we can win the court battles, but I'm sure of one thing: we won't win peace of mind.

In that kind of divorce, *nobody* wins.

My wife and I decided, fortunately, to separate with as little legal fuss and conflict as possible. Our story might have finished there, or with the finalization of the papers a year later, but if you have gone through a divorce, you know that the story doesn't have any simple end. Failed relationships leave behind a powerful residue of pain and sadness, distrust and doubt. I had already gone through that unpleasant cycle several times.

If I only knew one thing, it was that I damn sure didn't want to go through it again. I was reminded of the old saying about the definition of insanity: it's when you keep doing the same thing over and over, expecting different results.

If you're going through a divorce, I'm sure you don't want to experience all that pain again either.

If we want a better future, we have to make some sense of the past. We have to ask a fundamental question, one that might seem like a no-brainer: What are marriage and divorce really *about?*

♌

When *bad things happen to us* —that's how we usually see it— we tend to ask two questions.

Why is this happening?

And, *Why is this happening to me?*

For the first question, humans have managed to come up with all sorts of answers. We attribute our misfortunes to the actions of the gods, or the stars, or malevolent spirits, or scientific cause and effect.

The second question feels more urgent. Usually, we frame it with indignation: *Why is this happening to me, when I don't deserve it?* Sometimes, though, we ask it with a sense of shame. We suspect that bad things happen because there's something wrong with us.

Much of the time, I reasoned that my marriage had ended largely due to my wife's personal issues. The rest of the time, though, I burned with negative feelings about myself. Had she left because I was a bad person? Because I was an inherently angry person? Because I wasn't rich or successful enough? Because deep psychological failings prevented me from being able to manage a healthy relationship?

If I didn't want to put the blame on Claire or on myself, I could say that the marriage failed due to difficult circumstances, or irreconcilable differences, or even plain old bad luck. *Shit happens.*

My experience was hardly unique. Every day, thousands of marriages are ending all over the world. Every year, millions of people experience the pain of divorce. I could have simply written my story off as just one more case of love gone wrong. Thanks to my new exposure to Buddhism, though, I sensed that something deeper was really going on.

There was another story beneath the obvious one.

I went back and took another look at my little tale of woe.

At some point, presumably, the big man I saw in the real estate office had been happily in love with his wife. Now he was getting drunk, screaming at people, and punching holes in walls.

I thought of myself, feeling a rush of love as Claire walked out onto that waterfront pier on our wedding day, then cursing her as I walked through our half-empty apartment.

These stories seemed to be all about feelings. Marriage-and-divorce, the ultimate emotional crayon box. What a rainbow: infatuation, lust, yearning, love, kindness, compassion, bliss, dissatisfaction, jealousy, resentment, bitterness, anger, mourning, grief. . . . In the middle of a divorce, we may be reminded of the old saying, *There's a thin line between love and hate.* We stand together on one bright side of a line, and then somehow cross over into someplace dark.

If you think about it, though, a thin line between love and hate is a weird notion. Shouldn't those two emotions be separated by all the rest? Aren't they on opposite ends of a very wide spectrum?

Intuitively, though, it makes sense. There's some kind of powerful charged closeness of good and bad feelings in a divorce, a tangled braid, as if the more love you put into a marriage, the more anger and pain ultimately comes out.

That's confusing—and it's scary.

If love is something that can curdle overnight, like milk left out of the refrigerator, if it can just *go bad*, if marriage is that fragile and unstable, then it's like a nightmare.

We need to wake up.

The big question is, *How?*

you aren't my sunshine

As I explored Buddhism more deeply, I noticed that everyone kept talking about happiness.

I was surprised. I would have expected that Buddhist doctrine would look down on the desire for happiness and treat it as a low priority, something trivial compared to high-minded goals. Religion is about spiritual purity, right? It's about moral uprightness, and doing good deeds so you can get into heaven. What does mere happiness have to do with it?

But Matthew put it front and center in that very first talk. "Everybody wants the same two things. We all want to avoid suffering, and we all want to be happy." He didn't say that there was anything wrong with those fundamental wishes — in fact, he made it clear that Buddhism was designed to help.

As that message sank in, I began to think about divorce in a different light.

It goes without saying that our tale would sound different if Claire was the one telling it, but I suspect that the essential story line would remain the same: *I was looking for happiness; I thought I found it; I grew dissatisfied; I suffered.*

Like all divorces, then, this is a story about the search for happiness, and a story about suffering.

Wait a minute—haven't we just gone back to feelings?

As a matter of fact, no. As we're about to see, the search for happiness and the experience of suffering are really more about *thoughts*—and that's very good news.

We tend to think of emotions as states that arise inevitably in response to external events. *I can't help falling in love with you.... You make me angry.... I'm unhappy because my spouse is behaving badly....* If feelings are just reactions, then we seem to be at their mercy.

But if the real issue is what we're *thinking,* then we *can* do something about that.

We can learn to change our minds.

From a Buddhist point of view, if you can change your mind, you can change your world.

◻

As I went to more talks, I heard about all sorts of topics, but the underlying question was generally the same: *Where do happiness and suffering really come from?*

Let's start with suffering. From the very beginning, Buddhism was all about learning how to confront this affliction head-on.

The central figure of Buddhism lived in India 2,500 years ago. Siddhartha Gautama began his life as a prince. Before he was born, so the story goes, it was foretold that he would become either a great ruler or a great holy man. His father the king, eager for the boy to succeed him, shielded him from any religious teachings or evidence of suffering. The young prince lived a life of luxury and security, and was never allowed to see any sick or old people. The palace gardeners even crept out at night to remove any dead or dying blossoms from the grounds.

When Siddhartha was twenty-nine years old, he ventured outside the palace walls and saw four things that shocked his sheltered eyes: an old person, a sick person, a corpse, and a wandering monk. He suddenly became aware of old age, illness, and death, and he discovered the possibility of a different way to live. Instead of retreating into his palace, he was so moved by what he had seen that he resolved to spend the rest of his days learning about suffering. He left his safe life behind and embarked on a long spiritual quest. After years of wandering and wrestling with life's biggest questions, he finally reached enlightenment and became known as the Buddha, or Awakened One. (Talk about making a long story short!) He decided to spend the rest of his days passing on what he had figured out about how the world worked.

And what was his very first sermon about? He was able to sum up his message in just one sentence: "I've come to teach one thing, and one thing only: *suffering, and the end of suffering.*"

As Buddhist writer and meditation teacher Sharon Salzberg points out, his way of putting things seems odd. *Suffering; the end of suffering* — that's *two* things, right?

Actually, as she explains, they turn out to be inextricably linked.

The Buddha outlined the chief things he had learned in his search for enlightenment. He called them The Four Noble Truths.

The first was The Truth of Suffering.

Many people around the world today are terribly familiar with hard times, but here in the affluent West they tend to take us by surprise. I think it's fair to say that most of us think of suffering as a rude exception to the rest of our lives. We're cruising along, going to work, buying stuff, enjoying stable times, and then *Bam!* Something bad comes along. A friend gets diagnosed with cancer. Our company downsizes and we're laid off. A parent has a heart attack. Our marriage falls apart.

We're shocked and offended. This is not the way things are supposed to be! This is not the happiness and comfortable life we've been promised in every advertisement we've ever seen. We get angry and fight the news, or we deny it and get depressed.

In short, our shock, disbelief, and refusal to accept what happened increase the pain of the actual event.

Buddhism doesn't see suffering as something unusual. In fact, the First Noble Truth says that our worldly experience is *inherently unsatisfactory.* We experience moments of happiness, but they're inevitably overtaken by loss or change or sickness or old age or death. Suffering is not the exception — it's the rule.

Cheery, right?

In truth, the message is far from dark. Bear with me; we'll get to the good news soon.

The Second Noble Truth said that there is a *cause* for suffering.

In my case, I figured that the cause was obvious. *My wife left.* I had every reason to suffer.

Pop music certainly backed me up. Consider one of the most popular love songs of all time, "You Are My Sunshine," in which the singer explicitly equates his lover with his only chance for happiness.

My happiness had up and gone.

That explanation seemed self-evident, but it turned out to be a huge red herring.

According to the Buddhist way of looking at things, Claire's departure was hardly the root of my suffering. Suffering—so this argument goes—doesn't come from things that happen to us. It comes from the mistaken way we think about them. *You are my sunshine?* We sing along cheerfully, thinking this is a happy tune. From a Buddhist perspective, though, it's a disaster. I was beginning to realize that singing this song, metaphorically speaking, might even be a major cause of my suffering in the first place.

The Third Noble Truth? We're getting to the good part. The Buddha said that the *end* of suffering is actually attainable. No more worries, no more heartbreak, no more grief. (I should point out that we're not talking about the end of *pain*—even buddhas still feel that. The issue is how we *react* to pain.) The Buddha managed to end his own suffering, and he was not a god. He was just a human being, and he promised that anyone can achieve the same thing. That means *me*. That means *you*. Not in some future heaven. Not even in some future incarnation. Right here, right now.

ɑ

That might seem like a very airy promise, but he backed it up with the Fourth Noble Truth: there is a *path* out of suffering.

He even went on to spell it out.

part two

COME ON, GET HAPPY!

saturday night fever

If you're in the middle of a rocky marriage or a bitter divorce, I don't think I have to dwell on the First Noble Truth. You don't need to be convinced that life is not the proverbial bowl of cherries.

We're going to move on and try to figure out the real causes of our troubles. Once we identify them, we can work on doing things a better way. We can set off on a path out of suffering.

The essence of Buddhism is that it locates our problems not in the external world—my crummy spouse, bad luck, cruel fate—but in our own heads. Specifically, the Buddha warned about what he called The Three Poisons.

The first poison is *desirous attachment.*

That's a confusing term, and it's going to require some explanation. I'm going to introduce it by jumping ahead in my personal saga, to an event not explicitly mentioned in classical Buddhist scripture: The Hot Date.

I was walking to the subway and it was a cold evening in March, but it felt like spring to me. I strutted like John Travolta in *Saturday Night Fever*, only it wasn't the Bee Gees singing along in my private soundtrack; it was James Brown: "I Feel Good." And I *did*, too, better than I had in the past nine months. My entire body was shot full of endorphins. I was on my way to a date with a lovely woman, and our previous one had ended with a spectacular make-out session.

During the four and a half years I was with Claire, I hardly looked at other women, and can honestly say I never considered any type of affair. I was in love for life and didn't have a single regret about my commitment. I did occasionally miss one thing, though, something that marriage could never provide: this crazy first anticipation of romance, before reality catches up with the fantasy, when the whole world seems buzzing with a sugary rush of possibility. Even so, I was glad that I would never have to go through dating again: the pacing around, agonizing over whether to make that first call; the mind-numbing eternity of a bad blind date; the letdown of having to reject someone or be rejected.

For a while after my marriage ended, I couldn't even think about it. A couple of friends suggested that I get out into the social scene and enjoy being single again, but I didn't want to: it seemed like a betrayal of Claire, our union, our dream of a life together. I didn't want some fling with a stranger—I wanted my wife. The idea of opening up and trusting someone new gave me the serious heebie-jeebies. Even so, as the months went by, despite my new identity as the impervious Buddhist Man of Steel, the thought of a little human companionship and intimacy began to seem increasingly appealing. In a word, I got lonely.

I looked at online dating sites, and noticed that daters were supposed to post their relationship status: Single or Divorced. I was still having a lot of trouble mentally placing myself in that second category—why, I wondered, should I trumpet it to potential dates? (A friend, an experienced online dater, countered that putting myself in that category might not be a liability: it indicated that at least I had been willing to commit.)

As it turned out, I didn't have to go to much trouble. First, I encountered an old girlfriend at a party, and we had a brief but gratifying reunion. (It *was* possible to be intimate with someone else! All the equipment still worked!) Then my friends John and Lynne helped to arrange a date with a friend of theirs, who I'll call Tina. I had met her several years before. Here's a testament to the modern prevalence of divorce: we had once shared dinner, on a triple date. John was there with Lynne, I was there with Claire, and Tina was there with her own spouse. Two breakups later, now *we* were getting together.

Tina was very attractive and smart (a business professional, a real change for this artsy writer.) On our third date, she suddenly asked if I would mind if she kissed me. We had a great evening, which culminated in a hot time rolling around on her couch.

I was high as a kite.

◖

The next day, Tina went out of town, on a ski trip she had planned months earlier.

She was gone for a week. I e-mailed to say how much I had enjoyed our dates, but held off calling for a couple of days. (I didn't want to seem over-eager.) I was still enjoying that sugary buzz, but it started to fade. Finally, I called. I got Tina's voice mail and left a message. And then I waited.

And waited.

A couple of days went by.

My spirits took a dive. I began to feel rejected, and dejected, and I started to fill in Tina's silence with my own imaginings. *She doesn't really like me. She changed her mind, and she's bailing out. . . . She met some hotshot ski instructor, and they're making out in a hot tub right now . . .* I couldn't focus on my writing. I didn't feel like eating. I kept staring at the phone.

And I started getting angry. How dare she treat me in such an inconsiderate way!

Finally, Tina called back. We had a brief, hard-to-read conversation, but made a plan to get together when she got back. Now I was confused, seesawing back and forth between elation and doubt.

I felt, in short, like a teenager.

I wasn't a teen, though. I was an adult, and I had a brand-new way of making sense of what I was going through.

◌

Dating, like divorce, was turning out to be a powerful test laboratory for Buddhist insights.

Before, I would have believed that Tina's behavior was leading directly to my emotional states: that she was making me happy; that she was making me suffer.

Now I was able to interpret what had just happened in a very different way. I could step back, and even laugh at myself.

Here's a look at this experience from that new perspective.

My initial elation was fun, but misguided. I had just spent nine largely miserable months, and was more than ready for a little joy. I saw Tina as the person who could provide it, as if she was an intrinsic, guaranteed source of happiness. Sex had a lot to do with it. I didn't know much about her after just a couple of dates, not how kind she might be, or how much of a good sport in a crisis, but I knew that she appealed to me physically. She had a fine figure and was an excellent kisser. She could make me happy—or so I *thought*.

This seems like a good time to point out another popular fallacy about Buddhism: that it sees desire as the root of all suffering. I first came across that notion in high school, in some textbook on comparative religion, and I remember thinking, *What a drag.* I *liked* desire, and the last thing I wanted was to give it up. In fact, Buddhism doesn't call for a renunciation of all desire. I could point out, for example, that Buddhists say that it's great to desire to be enlightened, and to help others—but that sounds annoyingly goody-goody. In fact, Buddhism is not against making out, or ice cream, or any of our cherished delights. There's nothing inherently wrong with these things, as long as we see them clearly for what they are: simply sources of transitory pleasure. The trouble comes not with desire, but with *desirous attachment,* which causes us to see those things in a distorted way, to exaggerate their perceived good qualities, to get mentally agitated, to try to merge ourselves with them. Next thing we know, we're ruining someone else's marriage, or we're overweight, or addicted to some harmful substance, or in debt. In short, we're *suffering.*

If I chose to see Tina as an intrinsic source of my own happiness, I was setting myself up for a fall. She was an independent person, with her own wishes and desires, and inevitably those would come into conflict with my inflated expectations. That's exactly what happened. She didn't call back; I plunged into despair.

Because of my new ability to step back a little, though, my new attempts at mindfulness, I was able to see the situation more clearly. It was like peering into a scientist's high-powered microscope. Fascinated and amused, I watched my thoughts hurtle around like dizzy electrons in a cloud chamber. It wasn't my heart that was leading me astray, but the agitated workings of my *mind*.

How did I change my perspective and let go of my expectations? What happened when Tina came back from her trip?

I'll finish that story a little farther down the road.

happy hour

By using the example of a date, I may have given the impression that desirous attachment is mostly about sexual or romantic desire. In fact, it applies to a huge range of external objects.

As one of my Buddhist teachers pointed out the other day, we humans actually spend the bulk of our time on this planet, day in and day out, chasing after happiness, or at least comfort and satisfaction. We think something outside us will provide it, and we desire that thing.

Once we become aware of this pattern, it becomes glaringly obvious. We reach out for happiness on a small scale. We might wake up, thinking *Oh, I'd be so happy if I could just have a cup of coffee.* We drink a couple of cups, but then feel a bit jittery. Later in the day, we might think, *Oh, I would be so happy to sit down.* We sink into a chair, but then our back starts to hurt and we think, *I'd be happier if I stood up.* We get hungry, and think *It would be great to go to that new restaurant everybody's talking about.* We go there and discover that the food is overrated, or maybe the service is not so good. (Or maybe everything really *is* great—but we're hungry again a few hours later.)

We reach for happiness on a big scale too. We think, *I'll finally be happy when I get that other, better-paying job*—and then we find out that our new boss is a control freak, or we're asked to do something we don't feel is ethical. We think, *I'll be happy if I can only get that attractive person,* and then we start a relationship with them and discover that they're not very kind, or that we don't have much in common.

I began to notice something else. Our search for happiness tends to lead to the opposite of what we're looking for—to *dis*satisfaction. When we learn that our desired objects are not the fantasies we created in our minds—when, for example, we discover that our spouse is not our idealized perfect mate—then *bang!*, suffering results.

That doesn't stop us, though. When we find that things are not what we'd hoped they'd be, we move on to other things. (In the context of marriage, this phenomenon is called *divorce.*) The cycle never ends. It's like a bad magic trick, but we keep falling for it; despite countless experiences of disappointment in the past, we still cling to the hope that some new thing—or person—will bring lasting joy.

Unfortunately, our culture does everything possible to encourage that idea. If you turn on your TV right now, you'll see commercials saying that you'll feel braver and sexier and more secure if you buy a new car. If you turn on the radio, you'll hear love songs that say *I can't be complete without you.* If you go to your local newsstand, you'll see magazine after magazine plastered with beautiful people, trying to make you believe you'll be more content if you were thinner, less gray, better-dressed — if, in other words, you buy a new diet plan, or hair dye, or clothes.

Yet every thing we turn to has problems. Ice cream certainly seems like a solution, but if we eat too much we feel sick and we get fat. We can buy flat-screen TVs and SUVs, but they eventually wear out or break down. Fashion and cosmetics might make us feel more young and appealing, but wrinkles always win.

Here's an interesting question: What if happiness really *was* out there? What if the things we bought could really bring us durable joy and satisfaction? Imagine it — there you are, strolling along, and you see a great pair of shoes in a store window, and you stop in and try them on, and *Bingo!:* Lasting Happiness.

If that worked, you wouldn't need to buy another pair of shoes. Why bother? You'd already be happy.

Of course shoes can't ultimately make us happy, yet we keep buying more. Our economy is driven by this cycle of desiring, acquiring, and becoming dissatisfied. And consumer products aren't the only things that can wear out or grow stale. Even the ones that seem most wholesome and healthy, like a home, or friendships, are subject to change and loss. Marriages, sadly, are not exempt.

So what's the point? That we shouldn't have sex or eat ice cream or get married? That we'd be better off if we just lived alone, without any possessions, in a cave?

Not at all.

Just as our happiness is not inherent in external things, our suffering isn't inherent in them either. It arises from our mistaken reliance on them.

The idea is tricky. Again, the moral is not that desire is bad. I certainly desired my wife during most of our time together, and vice versa, and we felt happy when we brought pleasure to each other. There was nothing wrong with that.

And Buddhism is not saying that all attachment is bad. After all, parents have to feel attached to their kids. And if you want a marriage to work, you have to make a real commitment to your spouse.

The problem arises when we put the two together, when we become attached to things based on hopes for our own happiness. Maybe you've seen what happens when parents have kids just to make themselves feel good, or when you jump into a relationship that's based on what each partner can get out of it.

When we do that, and the other person doesn't fall in line and do the things that make us feel happy, we get disappointed, hurt, and angry.

It's not a thin line between love and hate. As we'll soon see, the Buddhist idea of love is not so fickle. In the meantime, we *can* say that there's a very thin line between desirous attachment and a disappointed heart. The stronger the attachment, the greater the subsequent crash.

Found a marriage on it, and the consequences will be dire.

attachment at first sight

In sexual and romantic relationships, desirous attachment can be a huge problem.

Here's another popular saying:

It was love at first sight.

That's pretty weird, when you stop and think about it. (And Buddhism is all about stopping to think about things we usually take for granted.) What does the phrase mean? Maybe we're talking about some mysterious spiritual communication that passes through the eyes of two people who have just met, a commingling of souls, but the key word here is *sight,* and how much can you really tell about someone by looking at them? You can't know if they're compassionate or generous or trustworthy or loyal. You can't tell if they're smart, or open to new experiences, or if they'd make a good parent.

You *can* tell if you're sexually attracted to them, and I was always amazed at how fast I could do that. I noticed that I could look at someone from a block away and instantly decide whether they appealed to me, physically speaking. I could walk into a party and glance around and immediately decide, *She's attractive. She's not. She's* too *attractive for me.* . . . That clearly had nothing to do with love, but a great deal to do with desirous attachment. I was looking at other people and immediately slotting them into categories by whether or not I thought they had the potential to make me happy.

How do we come up with such narrow slots, such very specific criteria? Unfortunately, it starts at an early age, when we see people on TV, in movies, in magazines, in advertisements, even in children's picture books. We learn what our culture considers "attractive." (That word is very telling, when you think about it.) When we get a little older, we learn to associate that constricted range of images with our own sexual pleasure. I wish we could undo that conditioning. What if we could spontaneously fall in love with someone's generosity, or their kindness? What if we didn't care if they were overweight, or too *this* or too *that?* Think how much human suffering would disappear overnight.

Sometimes, I discovered that a quick attraction just masked other deep needs. Here's another example from my new dating life.

Sherry was the most powerfully, unabashedly sexual woman I had ever met.

She was an artist, and a talented one. We met briefly at one of her shows. She had a lithe runner's body, a veil of lustrous red hair, and eyes that suggested hidden depths.

Her steely gaze seemed to open up just for me. A sexual electricity charged the air between us.

We made a plan to get together for coffee. At that first real encounter, we had only forty-five minutes before she had to run off to a previous appointment, but our conversation was deep. We discovered that we shared an interest in Buddhism. I told her about my divorce, and learned that she was considering ending a long-term relationship of her own.

After, we began to correspond by e-mail, and our online exchanges grew increasingly personal. Sherry seemed intensely interested in me, and I was definitely interested in return. When it became clear that our connection was about to really ignite, though, I backed off. I told her that since she barely knew me, it would be crazy for our fledgling attraction to serve as the catalyst for the end of her years-long relationship. (Sexual misconduct, especially interfering in someone else's relationship, is a big no-no in Buddhism. I was just starting to put my feet on my new spiritual path, and was not eager to veer off it so quickly and so hard. Aside from that, I knew what it felt like to have a woman leave me, and the last thing I wanted was to help drop the bomb on some other guy.) I told Sherry that she needed to resolve her situation based on its own merits, without considering me at all.

She agreed. And then she broke up with her partner. I told her that I thought we should wait a while to let that situation settle.

Finally, we were free to do what we wanted, two consenting adults. We got together, and the tinder exploded. I discovered that Sherry was absolutely frank and uninhibited about her desires.

There I was in the middle of my divorce: lonely and disoriented and low on self-esteem. Here came a woman who was talented, sexy, and passionate. It seemed too good to be true.

After a short time, I began to sense that it was.

Lesson Number Two from the Buddhist dating laboratory: *Our search for happiness is often really a flight from suffering.*

Aside from our e-mail correspondence, Sherry and I had only been together a handful of times. I was surprised by how enthusiastic she seemed about starting a relationship with me. Now, I'm not bad-looking, but I'm not George Clooney. I was flattered by the attention, but also suspicious. I began to feel that Sherry's intense interest was not really in me as a person; it seemed more about avoiding the pain of her last breakup. If she could get excited about getting together with someone new, she wouldn't have to spend time abiding with the guilt and disappointment of that failed relationship. And she had been with someone continually since she was in her early twenties; she was anxious about whether she could handle life on her own.

I started to feel as if I was a drug Sherry had sought out in order to avoid suffering. I couldn't blame her because I recognized my own past behavior, on a lesser scale.

(In any romantic situation, the difference between desirous attachment and real love may be hard to determine. Here's a simple litmus test: if you're feeling a lot of mental agitation, chances are it's the former. Why? Because, as Matthew explained in one of his talks, any time your mind is agitated, that indicates that there's a delusion present — you're setting yourself up in opposition to what's real, and that *hurts*.)

Luckily, since we were both somewhat familiar with Buddhist thought, I was able to explain my doubts to Sherry, to tell her that I felt uncomfortable about the situation. I backed away from our budding relationship. Sherry was not happy, but at least she was able to begin to do what she really needed to do for herself: to face her own groundless, challenging, yet hopefully rewarding new path.

In the last chapter, I talked about the many ways in which we seek out happiness. If you read that passage again, you'll notice that many of those moments of moving toward happiness are also moments of trying to jump away from uncomfortable feelings.

What's the most uncomfortable feeling of all? It's one of the main things that separates us from other animals: we're the only creature that knows it has to die. The result is a hugely powerful, mostly suppressed anxiety.

One of the most profound books I have ever read is called *The Denial of Death.* Written in 1973 by a cultural anthropologist named Ernest Becker, it argues that our shared fear has been one of the strongest driving forces in human civilization. We have built up many of our major social institutions in defense. Religion allows us to believe that we can surmount death by passing on to an afterlife. Through art we strive for a different kind of immortality. War gives us the strange, misguided notion that we can push death away by directing it toward others.

Whatever we do, our anxiety doesn't disappear.

Any time you want a vivid illustration of how it can control human lives, all you need to do is take a stroll through Manhattan's luxury shopping districts. Ultra-rich people drift through the stores like sharks who'll die the moment they stop buying. They've put a desperate faith in so many external things: in social status, in the accumulation of wealth, in the purchase of material objects, in trying to look good by buying expensive clothes, in trying to stay young through plastic surgery. All of this clearly doesn't work. The surgeries don't achieve the desired effect—their faces still look haunted, hollowed out by fear.

Fortunately, life has given us another antidote to this fear, something very powerful.

Let me give you a few hints:

It's a many-splendored thing.

It means never having to say you're sorry.

And it's all you need.

bollywood under
the bridge

If we're talking about happiness and suffering, and particularly about marriage and divorce, there's one question we clearly have to ask: What's love got to do with it?

We don't just say positive things about love. We call it strange, blind, a drug, a battlefield, and a four-letter word.

Which is it? Is it just a painkiller, another cheap escape from suffering, or something more substantial, maybe even a route to true happiness?

◑

I had cause to ponder the meaning of love one October afternoon.

I had a journalistic appointment down near the Brooklyn waterfront. After, I wandered aimlessly through the quiet old canyons of brick and cobblestone that surround the base of the Manhattan Bridge. I was in a sad mood, a contemplative mood; I was thinking about my impending divorce. I was in a private frame of mind, but then I entered a little park at the river's edge and came upon one of those bursts of activity — like a psychic eruption — so often pictured in movies by Federico Fellini.

A group of twenty people, mostly Indian, bustled around piles of technical equipment. Some spoke urgently into walkie-talkies, others gathered around a big movie camera, still others maneuvered a reflector screen that stood out against the backdrop of the East River like a sail. I had moseyed into the thick of a Bollywood film shoot.

Most of the crowd wore film-crew casual, high-tech anoraks and rugged sneakers, but one man stood out, and not just because of his different attire. In his immaculate cowboy boots and tight pressed jeans he stood taller than the others, and he had a sleek pompadour, soulful eyes, and the chiseled jaw of an Indian Marlboro Man. As one technician fussed about him, applying powder to his face, another handed him a fresh shirt. In one smooth gesture he pulled off his jersey, revealing the sculpted pecs of someone with a full-time private trainer.

It's a commonplace that movie stars are the avatars of the modern age, the embodiments of our need for mythic grandeur, and this guy certainly seemed larger than life, even offscreen. The funny thing, though, was that I had no idea who he was. For all I knew, I was right near the Indian Tom Cruise. (As I found out later, I *was.*)

While attendants darted in and out of his presence, this man from the Buddha's home country sat on a park bench a few yards away from me, staring manfully into the distance, toward the grand old span of the Brooklyn Bridge. A young Indian couple happened by and their eyes widened as they caught sight of him. The young woman fumbled for her cell phone to tell someone who she had just seen, while her boyfriend used his to snap photos. I could see how important this moment was to them, how it was elevating their blood pressure. I too had felt such distorting excitement in the presence of celebrities, that sense of being brought closer to some more powerful, essential VIP area of life.

Here, though, I didn't experience that vision-blurring awe. Because I had no idea who the man was, I was able to observe him with a detached eye. Snips of music blared out of P.A. speakers, and I knew that the actor was waiting for the moment when he would get to do his thing: he'd gaze deeply into the camera, move his pumped-up body in time with the music, and lip-synch about his undying love for some distant village girl.

I flashed back to a moment during my honeymoon. Claire and I had traveled to the Greek island of Santorini. Before it became almost completely overrun by cruise ships and by tourists in search of the perfect souvenir, it must have been one of the most beautiful spots on earth. The island is a circle, the high rim of a volcano surrounding a bowl of azure sea. Whitewashed dwellings hug the cliffs. Strip away all of the day-trippers clambering about with their digital cameras, and it would look like the serene, majestic place you see in travel posters. As we made our way along a narrow cliff-top, my wife and I came upon another Bollywood shoot, set up on the roof of one of those blindingly white-plastered homes. As the camera rolled and the playback played, a handsome Indian man lip-synched yearningly to a beautiful Indian woman. She shook a finger at him playfully, her supple body swathed in diaphanous veils that danced in the breeze.

Hollywood has long been the world's romantic dream factory, where the guy always gets the girl, but these days India is challenging that franchise. Most Bollywood epics follow a simple pattern: boy and girl fall in love; complications of caste or class separate them; they're finally reunited. Everybody sings, everybody dances. True love conquers all, and marriage soon follows. It's a difficult goal, but after it's reached everything extends into the future in a blissful haze. *Happily ever after.* The End.

I remember talking to married friends before I tied the knot myself. They spoke highly of their conjoined state, but invariably added one qualifying phrase: "It's hard work." I always found that puzzling. If you find your soul mate, and you're deeply in love, then you're finally happy, right? Why would that require *work?*

If you're married or divorced right now, you're probably chuckling at my naiveté, just as I chuckled recently during a media event featuring a writer here in New York. She had made a splash as a chastity advocate (not just for teenagers, but for all single people). She seemed to be arguing that saving sex for the context of marriage would automatically make it a hugely profound experience. The woman had never been married herself, and the way she spoke of the institution—as some sort of gauzy, idealized Shangri-la that would immediately confer a magic aura of protection, connection, and spirituality—seemed downright adolescent.

It was hard to blame her, though. Like her—like most people—I had grown up with a similar rosy ideal.

In the real world, though, spouses *never* come in an ideal, perfect form.

Back to the park bench.

I glanced over at the star sitting next to me. In a few months his handsome face would dominate movie screens around the world, and millions of women would swoon over it. Today, though, that face looked troubled. I soon found out why.

I had heard the young Indian couple mention his name, and when I got home I Googled him. It turned out that the icon had some big personal problems, including several pending lawsuits. Years earlier, he had allegedly been driving drunk in India when he careened up onto the sidewalk and killed one "pavement dweller" and injured four others. As if that weren't enough to crease his perfect brow, he was also charged with participating in a hunting incident in which two deer had been killed. Unfortunately for him, the deer were on the endangered species list.

Am I saying that we shouldn't get married because our spouse might turn out to be a drunk driver or killer of endangered animals? Of course not. But they *will* turn out to be less than ideal. Guaranteed. As my teacher Matthew put it, "The perfect person we thought we were getting together with turns out to be . . . a person. And we get angry." The more we fail to see that coming, the more disappointed we're going to be.

The problem here is not love itself; it's what happens when we chase some fairytale mirage of utterly fulfilling romance, when we view our "beloved" as someone who is going to take away our isolation/loneliness/suffering, and bring us big heaping platters of happiness—and isn't that the way we usually dream of love?

On an intellectual level, what I'm saying may seem obvious. We all know that "nobody's perfect." On an emotional level, though, we hold fast to our childhood fantasies. If we cling to an ideal of love that can't possibly exist in the real world—not consistently, not over the course of an entire marriage—we're setting ourselves up to suffer.

As we'll see a couple of chapters down the path, the problem with our usual notion of love is not just that it's unrealistic. There's a deeper flaw in it, one that often tears relationships apart.

nowhere to run

The Buddha spoke of three mental poisons that screw up our lives and cause us to suffer.

The first is desirous attachment, the delusion that causes us to see external things as inherent sources of happiness, to exaggerate their good qualities, and makes us want to grasp for and merge with them.

The second delusion also distorts our perception of external things, only this one, *aversion*, causes us to see them as inherently *un*desirable, and makes us want to move *away* from them. To observe the awesome destructive power of this delusion in the world, all you need to do is pick up a newspaper: you'll see anger, hatred, abuse, violence, and war.

These two poisons can be closely related. As we've seen, desirous attachment tends to flip, and nowhere is this more obvious than in a rocky marriage. If we're willing to believe that someone else is the source of our happiness, chances are we're going to be equally willing to believe that they're the

cause of our suffering. The almost violent desire of early attachment changes into a violent urge to push that person
away when things go bad. Likewise, the protective bond of
marriage, the commitment we make to be close to our
spouse, can start to feel suffocating, like a trap. A storm of
bad feeling is likely to erupt.

I'm thinking of a brutal movie scene I saw the other day.
I had rented a film called *Unleashed* to watch Jet Li, an
amazing practitioner of kung fu. Late in the story a bad guy,
also an ace martial artist, attacks our hero in an apartment.
They hurtle from room to room, snapping kicks and
punches and smashing all the furniture. Finally, they end up
pressed together in a narrow, closet-sized bathroom. Previously, Li has been able to use his acrobatic talents to leap
out of the way and escape his attacker, but now his sense of
options disappears. It all comes down to brute survival. The
fighting picks up in intensity and savagery as the two battle
like wild animals in a cage. The space is so small and con-
fined that it seems certain that only one combatant can
emerge alive.

We've all seen, heard about, or experienced divorces that
contained some of that churning, ugly energy, that destructive tornado powered by adrenaline and fear. I was lucky in
that my divorce contained more flight than fight, but I certainly felt the delusion of aversion coursing in my veins, and
I saw it operating in my wife. As I watched that furious
movie scene, I was reminded of something I had read about
divorce: "The suffering that comes from [marital conflict] is
painful enough, but as soon as you add the threat of losing
your children, your financial resources and your well-being,
the situation quickly becomes much worse. Now the situation is threatening. This potential loss of well-being can be a

serious threat to a person's survival. It can make a person fight as though his or her life depends on it. The moment this happens, the cycle of conflict escalates dramatically. . . . People become so full of fear, upset, anger and resentment, that they do horrible things to each other. The hurt and destruction are enormous."

The quote came from a website called *Divorce As Friends.* Its creator, someone named Bill Ferguson, had spent much of his career as a divorce lawyer, until he decided that he would rather help people heal their relationships. The site looked pretty commercialized, like a self-help infomercial touting a variety of tapes and other products, but it contained an article Ferguson wrote that explains the roots of divorce in a remarkably simple, direct, and insightful way.

He argues that as little children we are naturally able to feel emotional hurts and then let them go. Soon, though, we're taught to suppress those hurts and push them deep inside. Much later, in a marriage, our partner may do things that can subconsciously trigger those buried wounds, and the results can be ruinous. "Instantly," says Ferguson, "you become full of fear and upset. You get tunnel vision and lose your ability to see clearly. All you can do is fight, resist, hang on or withdraw. This hurt is responsible for all your suffering and all your self-sabotaging behavior."

Note that—like a Buddhist—Ferguson locates the suffering of a rocky marriage inside the mind of each partner, rather than blaming the other. I thought of the emotionally turbulent end of my marriage, in which Claire's willingness to take offense sometimes seemed far out of proportion to my actual behavior. Suddenly, her puzzling hypersensitivity made a lot more sense. I had been lucky enough to have a pretty emotionally stable childhood, but she had suffered some early traumas that left her with profound buried feelings of hurt. I failed to appreciate how much our disagreements triggered her old fears of anger and instability and loss. Evidently, she found those reactivated emotions unbearable.

Ferguson went on. "You create the experience of love by giving the gift of acceptance and appreciation. You destroy it by being judgmental, critical, and controlling. Notice how you feel when someone is non-accepting towards you. Notice how fast the experience of love disappears. Instantly, you get hurt. You get upset and close down. You put up your walls of protection and automatically become non-accepting and critical in return. Then the other person gets upset, puts up his or her walls of protection, and becomes even more non-accepting towards you."

That perfectly describes the unhappy downward spiral Claire and I locked into during our last weeks together.

"We think that we need to fight for protection," explained Ferguson. "We believe that if we just fight hard enough, then somehow, everything will get resolved in our favor. Not so. In fact, the opposite is true. The more you fight someone, the more of a threat you become to that person. You force that person to fight you even harder."

With my stupid insistence on proving myself right, I put more pressure on Claire. She didn't stick around to fight back.

Near the end of his article, as I'll soon relate, Ferguson describes a much more positive way to pull out of this desperate cycle of pain and rejection. I wish I had discovered his website before it was too late.

◻

As I mentioned earlier, I made new friends by going to Buddhist talks, and we found it helpful to share questions, advice, and—especially—doubts. Barbara, the sign designer, lived near me, and she often gave me a ride home. As we rolled through the dark Brooklyn streets, I would tell her about my struggles with my difficult feelings about my ex-wife, and she would ponder her long-term, sometimes-challenging current relationship. A small, spirited woman with a fantastic broad smile, Barbara brought to her three-year Buddhist practice a high level of engagement and determination. Her insights about the animosity between ex-lovers were typically perceptive and challenging.

"When I talk to two friends who have broken up," she said, "I often find that they have developed what I call an *enemy mind*. They loved each other, and now—all of a sudden—they're saying, 'That person was such a bitch!' For them to feel okay, the other person has to be the bad guy.

"I think that enemy mind comes out of a belief that the other person is trying to infiltrate and hurt you. We feel so vulnerable, but we don't know why—we're seeing everything in the wrong way. It's a huge mistake, but we think we're so at the mercy of external things. We think that everything around us dictates how we feel, and that everything that comes close is a threat. We attach our fear to something that shouldn't cause it—the person that's closest to us. They become the enemy because they're the person who might hurt us. There's a protect-myself-from-them state, a holding back.

"Buddhism changes everything," she said. "It shifts your worldview—you can't look at anything in the same way. Now I think, *What's the worst thing my partner can do to me: leave me?* Why am I so scared to let her in, to be vulnerable? It's not your partner who is going to hurt you, because suffering and happiness are *internal* experiences.

"We're longing for happiness and connection," she added, "but we actually rely upon delusions that cause the opposite: suffering and isolation. The delusional minds we go to for refuge, such as that enemy mind we spoke about, and anger, and jealousy, are the very causes for many of the relationship problems we have. We only rely on them because we have this mistaken view that they'll protect us from getting hurt. But—if we check—we can see that they're sources of suffering in themselves, and they just create more suffering."

who's number one?

We've already seen how much trouble desirous attachment and aversion can cause. As bad as they are, though, they're really just subsets of the third poison the Buddha warned about. If we look deeply into the many examples I've given thus far, we can usually find this root delusion lurking, determined to cause us pain.

Two people trapped in a narrow closet, fighting for survival. You Are My Sunshine. A childhood hurt. Love like a drug. Desperate shopping sprees. "I felt like the Incredible Hulk." A student with a full cup. She doesn't really like me. A man punching holes into a wall. You ruined my life, you bitch! A flare of anger in the post office. My need to be right. I Feel Good. "That place meant a lot to me." "I felt like I had been stabbed." You make me angry. You complete me.

What do they all have in common?

So far, I've used moments from my marriage and divorce as examples of how I came to internalize various Buddhist insights. This time, in order to introduce this insidious third delusion, the one that Buddhists call the source of literally all the unhappiness in the world, I'm going to go back in time.

Way back.

♦

I'm lying on my back in a dark room. I'd rather be on my stomach, but I can't push myself over, so I just wriggle uncomfortably. I hear a distant sound, but don't know where it's coming from—even in bright light, everything more that a foot or so away from me is just an indistinct blur. My little body is my world. A chafing in my thighs, a pressure of gas in my belly, air too chill on my skin—these are the most important things in life. Right now, there's a very agitated feeling in my stomach. I need food, and I need it now. Will it magically appear, or will I be left alone, lying here helpless? I open my mouth and begin to wail. I'm totally at the mercy of a couple of big, lumbering creatures who sometimes drift into my vision. Sometimes they come when I cry. Sometimes they don't. If I could form words, I would shout one panicked sentence into the dark:

WHAT ABOUT ME??

Decades later, I'm perfectly able to turn myself over in bed, or grab a snack from the refrigerator, but I still spend an inordinate amount of time walking around with that same question foremost in my mind.

If you check your own experience, you'll see that you do the same. Unless you're a buddha, you probably spend a good part of your day—maybe even the biggest part—thinking about yourself. *I'm feeling a little tired. What am I going to eat for dinner? Does he really like me, and will he call me again? My boss is going to be pissed off if I show up late tomorrow. I really should exercise more. Is that a new freckle on my shoulder, or could it be something worse? Am I ever going to find a job where my true talents will be put to use?*

Just as our whole experience of the world is filtered through our senses and our minds, so the world seems to revolve around us.

Maybe we're willing to widen that circle a bit. Maybe we say, *My family is very important.* Maybe we extend it even further. *My friends are valuable. My tribe or race or ethnic group is the best.* Even so, there's just one center of these concentric rings: Me.

We tend to organize our lives around our wish to avoid suffering and find happiness. Who are we seeking that happiness for? As Matthew pointed out in a recent talk, we might as well walk around carrying big placards proclaiming our guiding philosophy: Happiness For *Me* Now!

Don't believe we're that selfish? Let me ask a question: If you knew that you could give up your life to save ten random strangers, would you do it? How about a hundred other people? How about a thousand? Where would you draw the line?

Maybe there are times when you might sacrifice yourself to save just one other person. Many parents would do such a thing for their children. Some of us would do it to save a beloved spouse or sibling. Would we do it to save someone else's spouse or sibling, though? When you get down to it, my spouse and my sibling are so important to me because they're *mine*.

When one of our fellow humans lets go of this self-centered thinking, it makes news.

On January 2, 2007, a construction worker named Wesley Autrey was waiting for a subway train in Manhattan when he saw a man named Cameron Hollopeter suffer a seizure and fall onto the tracks. Despite the fact that a train was already roaring in to the station, Autrey leapt down, covered the other man with his own body, and kept him out of harm's way as the train thundered overhead. The train passed so close over Autrey that it left a grease mark on his blue knit cap. Autrey was fifty years old; Hollopeter was twenty. Autrey was a black man; Hollopeter was white. The two had never met. Autrey could easily have made a snap judgment: *this stranger is not part of my circle.* Instead, he saw a fellow human being in danger, and he risked his own life.

"I don't feel like I did something spectacular," Autrey said later. "I just saw someone who needed help." Of course, he was wrong; what he did *was* spectacular. It was a rare event, so shocking that it made international headlines. Autrey forced us to ask ourselves a very tough question: Would I be able to do the same? His brave gesture cut to the core, and made us see how hard we cling to our all-important selves.

ɔ

The notion that *I'm most special* feels so natural that we often don't see how it gets us into a world of trouble. In fact—and it takes considerable contemplation to see the truth of this— Buddhism points to it as the root of *all* human suffering. Anger arises out of it (due to the sense of personal injury). Desirous attachment arises out of it (due to the sense that our own needs are paramount.) So do a host of other delusions, from jealousy to racism, stinginess to greed. Buddhists call this dangerous delusion *self-cherishing.*

It's part of a larger problem, the Third Poison, the Big-Daddy delusion of them all: *ignorance.* Again, the term is a bit confusing. We're not talking about what we *don't* know, but what we mistakenly think we *do*. And we certainly think we're Number One.

Remember how I promised to point out another major flaw in our usual idea of love? This is it.

Think of popular professions of "true love." (I'm writing this a week before Valentine's Day, and the air is blizzarding with them.)

You're my everything.

You complete me.

I can't live without you.

What are these sayings really saying?

"My."

"Me."

"I."

Is the message *I love you*?

Not even close. It's *I need you to make me happy*.

When someone else fails to go along with the program of "making" us happy, we decide that they're a problem. We may decide that we don't like them. We may even choose to believe that there's something *inherently* unlikeable about them.

When someone contradicts our desires, when they hold up their own Happiness For *Me* Now! placard and it blocks ours, we tend to feel threatened, defensive, and angry. Our sense of self actually intensifies. Think of how easily this can happen. You're walking down the street and someone accidentally brushes against you, and you think, *Who does this guy think he is, invading my space like that?* You're driving and someone—accidentally, perhaps—cuts you off. You become indignant: *How dare this creep jump in front of me?* Your sense of self-importance flares up like a cobra's hood.

I think back to moments in my marriage. When our living situation was stable, Claire and I got along very well. But when I knew that we had to move, my attachment to my old place was so deep that I felt vulnerable and at risk. When Claire didn't like a new apartment I suggested, or I didn't like one that she preferred, I took those disagreements as personal threats. When that financial matter arose, my sense of self felt deeply wounded.

And when we had to negotiate conflicts, I was a lousy listener. I think of a classic Gary Larson *Far Side* cartoon. In the first panel, titled What We Say to Dogs, a man berates his pet: "Okay, Ginger! I've had it! You stay out of the garbage! Understand, Ginger? Stay out of the garbage or else!" In the second panel, What They Hear, the dog receives this message: "Blah blah Ginger blah blah blah blah blah blah blah blah Ginger blah blah blah blah blah. . . ." That's funny, but not when applied to a marriage. Like the dog in the cartoon, I tended to hear things in my interchanges with Claire only as they related to my cherished self. I fought to satisfy my needs, when I should have been fighting for *us*.

Actually, from a true Buddhist perspective, I should have been fighting for *her*.

Buddhists use another analogy to describe self-cherishing. Imagine that you're alone in a rowboat in the middle of a lake. You're lying on your back, looking up at the sky, and you can't see over the sides of the boat; you're just drifting contentedly. Suddenly, another boat comes along and smacks into yours. You immediately become angry at the other boatman or woman. (Or maybe you become depressed by their bad treatment of you. Either way, the essential thought is, *How dare they do this to me?*) You jump up, and look into the other boat — and discover that it's *empty*. Notice what happens to your sense of wounded self: it *shrinks*. You're able to calm down, relax, and lighten up.

Here's the interesting thing: even when we think that someone else *is* in the other boat — in divorce, for example — we can still learn to let go of our anger, to see that their intention is not necessarily to cause us suffering or harm.

Our sense of wounded self doesn't just result in anger. Pay attention next time you feel lonely or sad. One thing you'll probably notice is that your sense of self grows enormously. There's that timeless old cry swelling in the back of your throat: *What about me?* Later in the book, you'll find a number of interviews with other people who have used Buddhism to transform their experience of divorce. One of them notes that as a young woman she underwent intense periods of depression. Later, she came up with this acute observation: "Even *low* self-esteem is self-cherishing."

We can learn to take the focus off ourselves, though, to adopt a broader view. Jean Smith recounts a story about Buddhist teacher Chögyam Trungpa. Once he held up a big white sheet of paper on which he had drawn a small floppy "V." He asked his students to describe the picture. They all said that it represented a bird flying across the sky. "No," he replied. "It is a picture of the sky, with a bird flying across."

We limit ourselves in the same way. We identify with one little bird named *me*, when we could be connecting with the whole open sky.

When we begin to notice how pervasive self-cherishing is, we can see how much damage it causes, from broken marriages to the fact that people are often willing to literally slaughter others who threaten their sense of self (we call this dangerous egotism "war," and tend to glorify it by saying that it's a matter of "patriotism"). Clearly, we need to give it up.

Maybe you've already guessed where this is heading. As the eighth-century Buddhist sage Shantideva put it in his seminal book *The Way of the Bodhisattva*, "All the joy the world contains has come through wishing happiness for others. All the misery the world contains has come through wishing pleasure for oneself."

According to Buddhism, we not only should learn to see others as if they were as important as ourselves; we should see them as *more so.*

At this point, if you're like me, you may be harboring some serious reservations. Sure, I mail off a check to charity every once in a while, I volunteered for a tutoring program, I give change to homeless people. But to live as if other people were more important? You'd have to be a kind of saint, right? You'd have to give away most of your possessions. You probably couldn't enjoy dancing, or sex, or a good joke, or an occasional frosted malt beverage. I can feel my body growing heavy, just writing about it.

To be honest, this spiritual path is suddenly starting to sound as joyous as eating library paste.

danger, will robinson!

The problem looks glaringly simple.

If we turn away from our usual project of trying to make ourselves happy, and focus instead on the happiness of others, it seems logical that we'll have to sacrifice a lot of our own joy. Let me be honest here: I don't want to do that. I *like* my happiness, and I'm sorry, but I don't want to give it up for the sake of some dour moral crusade.

Earlier, we talked about the real meaning of love, and decided that *I need you to make me happy* just didn't cut it. So what's the Buddhist definition? Here's Geshe Kelsang Gyatso weighing in: "Love is a mind that appreciates another, cherishes them, and wants them to be happy."

Yikes.

That sounds very noble and generous, but at this point, I'm like the cranky old robot on *Lost In Space,* waving my metal arms frantically, chanting "Danger, Will Robinson!" This definition doesn't mention my needs at all. In fact, it doesn't even talk about some sort of mutual, reciprocal bond, none of the *we* that my couples therapist focused on.

Objections pop up immediately. What if I manage to generate this utterly selfless, other-cherishing love, and I give it to my partner, but she doesn't give it back? What if she treats me badly? Am I supposed to sit there, smiling blissfully, still offering my pure appreciation like some sort of dope? What about fairness? What about justice?!

Okay, *breathe*. Here I am, getting all worked up over a hypothetical situation. What does Matthew always tell me? "Don't just accept what I'm saying. Test it against your own personal experience and see if it works for you."

When I think about things a little more clearly, I have to admit that I've already tested the me-based approach to love. It didn't work out too well. It tended to make me uptight, defensive, demanding, and — ultimately — disappointed. It was a disaster.

In reality, though, most of my marriage was not a disaster at all. I hope I haven't made it sound as if it was a shallow relationship, founded only on the shaky basis of desirous attachment and self-cherishing. In fact, I remember many times of deep mutual happiness. During my best times with my wife, we realized that if we concentrated on pleasing each other, our love circled back — we *both* benefited. We even made up a name for this phenomenon: "the loop that glows." Yes, there were selfish times, especially at the end, but our marriage was also full of a love that was real.

Let's take another look at what Shantideva said.

"All the joy the world contains has come through wishing happiness for others."

He's not just talking about joy for those on the receiving end. At the times when I wished for Claire's happiness and acted upon that wish, I didn't feel deprived at all. Giving love away didn't deplete my store of pleasure; it *increased* it. I felt good about myself, less alone, more connected to life. As Matthew put it in a talk the other day, "Our isolation causes so much existential pain, but our loving others brings us so much happiness." Instead of making me feel neglected, gloomy, or heavy, I felt *lighter* at those loving moments, *more* fulfilled. "We're taking the focus off ourselves," Matthew added. "In truth, we're *sick* of ourselves." When we put the focus on someone else, we release ourselves from the boundless anxiety that accompanies our eternal *What about me?*

Think about that. Doesn't it sound good?

Some people think that if you get deeply into Buddhism, you're supposed to renounce all worldly pleasure, give away your possessions, and spend the rest of your life in a cave, or trek around holding out a beggar's bowl. In fact, the Buddha tried that route. He left his lavish life, joined up with some wandering ascetics, ate nuts and berries, and wore skimpy robes despite the cold. Did this grim path lead him to enlightenment? No—in fact, he became sick and malnourished. It almost killed him.

On the other hand, he knew that a pleasure seeker's life wouldn't bring enlightenment either. He had experienced that too: he had grown up in a swank palace and enjoyed great food, fine wine, and the company of some of the most sensual young hotties of his day.

Ultimately, he decided that the path to enlightenment should steer between attachment to pleasure and attachment to austerity. He called it The Middle Way. He said that you don't have to become a monk or nun to reach enlightenment.

You could incorporate his teachings into a normal life as a bricklayer or merchant, as a spouse and parent.

This idea of a middle way might sound like it would take a lot of fun out of life. Sure, it would be nice to get rid of the lows, but wouldn't it also cut out the highs? This is yet another misconception about Buddhism: that it leads to a narcotized, unpassionate indifference, a kind of Soviet-style enforced emotional mediocrity. In fact, Buddhism has nothing to do with eliminating sexual pleasure, or sensual joys, or romance, or anything like that. The antidote to attachment is not *detachment;* there's nothing in Buddhism that says that you're not supposed to care about life, about other people, about love. The Buddha promised that the path to enlightenment, far from being a gloomy plod toward sainthood, could be the source of great bliss.

His message was loud and clear: if you love others, you won't just contribute to their happiness—you'll increase your own.

◁

Fine and dandy.

In a better world, we'd all give up our selfish crusades, love others tirelessly, and everyone would dance together, holding hands in joy.

In real life, though, every marriage contains a tangled blend of real love and self-cherishing. Things are going great for a while, and then conflicts pop up, jolting us out of our generosity, reminding us of our own powerful needs and desires. A fuse blows and suddenly the circuitry of the loop reverses, from positive to negative.

How do we come to terms with that?

Recently, a woman I was casually dating sold her apartment and had to find a new place to live. The way she went about it seemed crazy to me.

When I look for an apartment, I try to carefully consider my budget; evaluate possible neighborhoods in terms of their crime rate, shopping options, restaurants, and closeness to the subway; and check to make sure there are no noisy neighbors or other potential problems. I tromp around for weeks.

What did my friend do? She looked at a few listings online, saw a picture she liked, a sublet, and went to talk to the owner, a woman about her age. They shared a nice chat and a couple of glasses of wine, and then my friend pulled out her checkbook and wrote out a deposit. She hardly knew anything about the neighborhood—and ignored the fact that she would just have to move again in six months—but she liked the apartment, she liked the owner, and that was good enough for her.

Did I argue with her? Did I get upset?

Not at all.

Why?

Because it wasn't my problem.

Instead of getting uptight about her different approach to life, as I had done with Claire during our own apartment search, I was able to shrug it off. The fact was, I didn't have to live there. I could appreciate and enjoy this woman's company on our occasional dates, and I didn't have to feel threatened by her way of doing things.

Despite what I saw as her impulsiveness and lack of judgment in picking the apartment, she seemed quite happy with it. We're back to our original anecdote of the gum-popper on

the subway. What seemed like an inherent problem, could—
if looked at from another angle—turn out not to be a problem at all.

Of course, if I had been married to her, I would have
found it a lot harder to adopt such a carefree attitude. I
would have had to live in that same apartment, and any un-
foreseen difficulties would have become mine as well. I
would likely have become disappointed or upset.

So what's the moral of the story?

It would be easy to conclude that the best way to find
serenity is to detach from other people and avoid relationships, which constantly push us into feeling challenged or
threatened. That argument feels especially convincing in the
aftermath of divorce, when the prospect of trusting and rely-
ing on someone new seems fraught with peril. *(Just when I
finally managed to put myself back together, how can I risk getting
blown to smithereens again?)* Anyhow, isn't the spiritual path
usually a lone individual journey, a process of splitting away
from the rest of humanity, like Moses climbing his mountain,
or Buddha going off to sit under his bodhi tree?

We could certainly cruise through the rest of our lives
avoiding real relationships. Unfortunately, we'd also have to
renounce exploring a deeper intimacy, sharing life's troubles
and joys, and giving and receiving true romantic love.

That seems like a lot to miss.

There's another reason to seek out a deep romantic bond,
though, one that has nothing to do with sex or comfort or
even love. In her book *Everyday Zen*, Buddhist teacher Charlotte Joko Beck has this to say:

> . . . as we endeavor to practice with relationships,
> we begin to see that they are our best way to grow.

In them we can see what our mind, our body, our senses, and our thoughts really are. Why are relationships such excellent practice? Why do they help us to go into what we might call the slow death of the ego? Because, aside from our formal sitting [meditation], there is no way that is superior to relationships in helping us to see where we're stuck and what we're holding on to. As long as our buttons are pushed, we have a great chance to learn and grow. So a relationship is a great gift, not because it makes us happy—it often doesn't—but because any intimate relationship, if we view it as practice, is the clearest mirror we can find.

Maybe a big part of the solution here is to stop looking at marriage as just a happiness-for-me machine. An essential message of Buddhism is that the tough times are a valuable part of the deal—that, as twelfth-century sage Geshe Chekhawa put it, we can learn to "transform adverse conditions into the path to enlightenment." Like parenting, a relationship can help us to reduce self-cherishing, to escape the exhausting treadmill of our own desires and demands.

We can seek relationships not because they're easy, or always satisfying, or guaranteed to make us happy.

We can welcome them, in all their messy, imperfect, frustrating glory, because they're a perfect field for spiritual growth. (That sounds a little groovy, but hey, if it's true, it's true.)

When I look back on my marriage, I have a lot to regret. I regret the way I sometimes behaved; I regret the way Claire sometimes behaved. And there's a lot I miss: love, sex, companionship, the potential for a family, stroking my wife's back late at night, some amazing homemade pies. . . . One thing I remember is that I often felt that marriage—that Claire—brought out the best in me, helped me to become a better person. I hope she felt that way about me sometimes.

I have no way of knowing what might have happened if we had stayed together—and I have to acknowledge that sometimes it might be healthier for both people in a marriage to go their separate ways—but I wish we had given our union a better chance. My biggest regret is not the love or the sex or the pies; it's that we both lost out on a major opportunity. If we could have just ridden out the difficult times—if we could have seen them as a chance to figure life out better—we might have become something truly incredible.

Together.

# of chambermaids and kings

Q: What did the Buddhist say to the hot dog vendor?

A: Make me one with everything.

It would be nice if I could promise that this book offered some kind of get-enlightened-quick scheme that could jump us to a fully selfless, blissful plane, but that's not the goal here. I'll be content if we can take a few small steps and make some actual progress toward a better divorce, and toward better future relationships. And—as Pema Chödrön puts it—we need to start from where we are: we're human beings afflicted with overbearing desires and aversions and a powerful sense of self. The good news is that we don't have to transform ourselves overnight—we can take those little steps, and see if we're moving in a helpful direction.

Where to begin? How can we move from our usual anxious, self-cherishing, relationship-sabotaging orientation toward a lighter, more compassionate way of relating to someone else?

Ultimately, the question is not just how we can love one other person better—it's how we can relate better to everyone else in the world.

That seems like a much higher mountain, but it might be a simpler place to start.

It's easy to think of Buddhism as a narcissistic, inward-focused religion. We picture someone sitting in lotus position, eyes closed, tuning out the world and its many problems. (Thus the uncomplimentary term *navel-gazer.*) In truth, there are schools of Buddhism that focus mostly on personal enlightenment, but the tradition I've been mainly influenced by, Mahayana Buddhism, emphasizes—over and over—that the point of becoming enlightened is that it enables you to help other people. There's a long tradition of *bodhisattvas*, people who—after great effort and struggle—attained enlightenment and were finally free of the cycle of worldly suffering. They could easily have said *adios amigos* to the rest of us poor bastards, but they stuck around because they wanted everybody else to experience the same freedom.

The Dalai Lama is a great example of a Buddhist who extends his compassion out into the world. In *The Art of Happiness: A Handbook for Living,* psychiatrist Howard Cutler relates a very telling story. The spiritual leader had come to speak to a gathering in Tucson, Arizona, and was staying at a big, fancy hotel. His first morning there, he emerged from his suite, followed by his usual retinue of assistants, bodyguards, journalists, etc. Out in the hallway, he encountered a chambermaid. She didn't know who this stranger was, in his foreign robes, but she figured that—judging by his entourage—he must be someone very important. That's why she was surprised when he stopped in front of her. He looked her directly in the eye, without any condescension, and offered a heartfelt Hello. The next morning when the Dalai Lama emerged from his suite, there were two maids waiting to wish him good morning. By the end of the week, when he was ready to check out of the hotel, dozens of maids were lined up to say goodbye.

Being nice to a few chambermaids might not seem like a very big deal. It took the Dalai Lama very little time or effort to acknowledge them and show them some respect. In another sense, though, what he did was exceptional. From what I've heard, he makes the effort to treat *everyone* this way. We're talking about a Nobel Laureate, head of a planet-wide community, a man who regularly hobnobs with world leaders, but he doesn't distinguish between chambermaids and kings. His friendliness might seem like a throwaway gesture, the kind any politician might make in order to impress visiting journalists, but in his case it's an expression of a fundamentally, radically different way of seeing the world: he truly believes that all people are inherently equal, and that outlook has helped make him one of the most beloved leaders of our time.

Attaining that level of compassion and generosity may seem very daunting, but you can easily begin to follow his example. The next time you get on a bus, give a direct, sincere Hello to the driver. When you buy a newspaper, don't just fork over some change and rush away; offer the vendor a sincere Thank You. And the next time you pass a homeless person on the street, take a second to look them in the eye and acknowledge that they're a fellow human being.

We have dozens of little contacts like this every day, and every one of them is an opportunity to practice generating a mental state that might be of great help the next time you find yourself in an argument with a loved one, or sitting across a lawyer's conference table from your ex. This mind is a medicine that counters the poison of self-cherishing; it's called *compassion*. My dictionary defines it as "sympathy for the suffering of others, often including a desire to help."

A few weeks after my marriage ended, I stopped in for lunch at an old Manhattan coffee shop. The counterman, a burly guy wearing a blocky paper hat, was a talkative sort; within two minutes he was telling me about his second job. Within five minutes he told me that his wife had recently died in his arms. "She had an aneurysm," he said as he sliced my tuna fish sandwich. "One minute she was here; the next she was gone."

Under normal circumstances, I think I would have felt uncomfortable at being told such an intimate story, as if a stranger had sat too close to me on a park bench. As it was, though, I understood. The man had gone through a heartrending experience, and the memory sat uneasily within him, and the only way to find relief seemed to be to get it out.

I was reminded of a sad little Chekhov short story called "Heartache." On a dark snowy night, a hansom cab driver whose son has just died of a fever tries to tell his fares about his misfortune, but they're so wrapped up in their own lives that they can spare him no sympathy or interest. One after another, they curse at him to pay attention to the road and drive on. He tries to tell his fellow cab drivers, but they don't want to hear his story either. "Isn't there someone among those thousands who will listen to him?" writes Chekhov. "If his heart were to burst and his grief to pour out, it seems that it would flood the whole world, and yet no one sees it." The old man ends up telling his sad story to his horse.

New York is a city of eight million people, and normally I put up firm walls to keep the others out. After my marriage died, though, I found that my experience seemed to open me to recognizing the sadness of others. Instead of making me want to recoil or ignore their pain, it made me feel closer to them. And I found myself acting a little kinder. Instead of feeling annoyed when I saw some panhandler who looked relatively healthy — *Why doesn't he just go out and get a goddamn job?* — I gave a buck. I figured that he wasn't getting rich begging out on the streets, and that even if he was, what difference did it make? I was learning to open my heart. Instead of ignoring appeals from charities as junk mail, I started sending off more checks. I made an active effort to offer support to people I met who were going through divorces or other hard times.

Friedrich Nietzsche said that what doesn't kill us makes us stronger, but it seemed that something else could also be true: What doesn't kill us can make us *kinder.*

the couch and
the cushion

All the Buddhist talk about suffering might seem rather depressing, but I found it comforting. It implied that I was not alone, or a freak, or inherently defective. I wish that psychotherapy had made me feel the same.

For seven months before our split, mostly at my wife's urging, I had been seeing a therapist. (And Claire was seeing one of her own.) Once a week, I dutifully made the trek up to the Upper West Side, the psychoanalysts' Promised Land. I entered a big old prewar building, signed in with the doorman, then rode up in the elevator, rehearsing what I was going to say about the past week's events. I'd slip into my therapist's anteroom and sit there nervously flipping through *People* magazine, or speculating about the hidden Rorschach meanings of the paintings on the wall. I'd politely pretend that I was unable to see the other patients who came walking (or rushing) out of his office when their forty-five minutes were up.

When my turn came, my therapist would politely usher me in, and I would sink into the obligatory Big Leather Armchair. I'd exchange a few pleasantries with him—he seemed like a nice guy—and then I would trot out my issues for the week. When I ran out of material, we'd stare at each other. *Am I boring him?* I wondered. *He keeps looking at the clock. Does he like me, or does he just seem friendly because he's paid to be?* I'd sneak my own glances at the clock, worrying—even though he had generously given me a struggling writer discount— about how our sessions were impacting my finances. I'd try to get past my own defensively preprepared material, and every once in a while we'd have a session that seemed to reach a deeper level. The premise of our talks seemed to be that I needed to understand and emotionally come to grips with my personal psychological problems. I needed to figure out how my early childhood experiences had molded and shaped—no, *mis-shaped* me. Forty-five minutes later, I'd scoot out past some other patient waiting with eyes averted, and I'd go and wander through nearby Central Park, trying to clear my head. I often ended up feeling vaguely uneasy, and isolated, and alienated.

I never felt that way after the Buddhist talks.

My point here is not to knock therapy. Seven months of once-a-week visits is not much time, and I likely didn't put enough energy into making real progress. I know therapy is helpful for a variety of psychological disorders, I know people who've benefited greatly from it, and I've had useful experiences of my own. The problem was, though, that I didn't have time for a leisurely course of sessions.

My marriage was going down in flames.

I'm reminded of a story about the Buddha and a man who had been shot by a poisoned arrow. When a doctor came, the wounded man refused to let him remove it, saying that first he wanted to know the age, caste, height, name, and hometown of the archer, not to mention the kind of bow and the origin of the feathers on the arrow. The Buddha said, "Surely the man will die before he knows all this." The first step was to simply pull the arrow out.

Likewise, my marriage was in a rocky place, and a more direct approach would have been a big help. How to improve a relationship is not some arcane mystery. Marriage requires a set of skills, and every marriage doesn't have to reinvent them from scratch. The information is readily available, if we take the trouble to seek it out. Some of it might come from Buddhism. Some might come from self-help books or even TV talk shows. Some might be passed on by older folks who have survived difficult times. It doesn't matter what the source is, as long as it helps.

For example, I had long been vaguely aware of a book called *Men Are from Mars, Women Are from Venus*. I never looked at it because I assumed that it was just cheap pop psychology, an airport read. After my marriage ended, though, a friend pointed me to a particular chapter. Author John Gray described a source of marital trouble that reminded me of one of the worst fights of my marriage.

I was having a hard time with my writing career. (A freelancer's income is notoriously unsteady.) One night, Claire suggested that I seek out more reliable ways of making money, such as teaching or editing. She kept pressing the point. I felt insecure and threatened, then cornered, and— finally—very upset. I ended up shouting at her.

I wish we had read Gray's chapter first. He explained that women sometimes offer career advice in a spirit of loving kindness. Men, unfortunately, are conditioned to interpret such counsel in a very different way. We don't hear, *I love you and I want to help.* Instead, we hear, *I doubt your competence and don't trust your ability to provide.* If Claire and I had known that, we could have spoken to each other in a way that would have led to a much more positive result. (Another good source of information about gender differences is Deborah Tannen's *You Just Don't Understand: Women and Men in Conversation.*)

After my marriage fell apart, I started seeking out that kind of information, but it was too late. While I still had time, I wish someone had simply said to me, "Here's how you can screw up a marriage. And here are some specific things that you can do to avoid that."

In any case, the Buddhist talks were a completely different experience. First of all, I wasn't closed off in a room with just one other person; I was sitting with a group who had come together in search of answers. And nobody was asking about my personal situation, my unique problems. Nobody, in fact, was talking about me at all. From the beginning, the focus was on our shared problems. Not on our problems as neurotic Americans; our teachers emphasized that we had common problems as *human beings.* "Everybody wants to avoid suffering. Everybody wants to be happy." They really meant *everybody:* Americans, Tibetans, Israelis, Palestinians, blacks, whites, women, men . . .

That emphasis on shared human desires and difficulties, rather than individual neuroses, made a lot of sense to me. We're not just suffering because our parents might have made mistakes. We've all had the same difficult experience of birth. We all experience aging and sickness. And we all know—hard as we try to repress and deny it—that we're going to die. We think that money or fame will elevate us above that fundamental worry, and we're jealous of people who possess those things, yet Donald Trump and Britney Spears are going to grow old and die just as surely as the servants who scrub their toilets.

Okay, so maybe all this talk of suffering *can* get a bit depressing, but the Buddhist talks gave me a sense of solidarity. At least I wasn't suffering alone.

That cheered me up a bit. Something else I heard cheered me up a lot more.

gold in the dirt

I went to my first Buddhist talk figuring that the essence of the approach would be *transformation* — that after a lifetime of self-denial and humorless austerity, I might hope to eventually become someone else, someone "enlightened."

Once again, I was utterly wrong.

Buddhism starts with a staggeringly different premise: that everybody, without exception, is already intrinsically *all right*. That we're all enlightened beings, inside. We don't have to buy anything, or renounce all our earthly possessions, or shave our heads and become monks and nuns, or trek to the Himalayas in order to find nirvana. We shouldn't have to do anything, or go anywhere to reach it.

Buddhism says that we all have a profound interior core of goodness and light called "Buddha nature." And we don't have to wait until we die and get to heaven to find it. It's here now, completely available to us at all times. What prevents us from doing so is our ignorance, which leads to our delusions, which obscure that inherent light.

Geshe Kelsang Gyatso has this to say about the subject: "Buddha compared our Buddha nature to a gold nugget in the dirt, for no matter how disgusting a person's delusions may be, the real nature of the mind remains undefiled, like pure gold. In the heart of even the cruelest and most degenerate person exists the potential for limitless love, compassion and wisdom. Unlike the seeds of our delusions, which can be destroyed, this potential is utterly indestructible, and is the pure, essential nature of every living being."

To put it in modern terms, we're like computers that come from the factory with excellent hard drives. The problem is that—all too often—we're operating on faulty software, which tells us, *Grab outside yourself for happiness! Think that it's all about you! Get angry or sad whenever you feel hurt!* If we could get rid of these corrupted instructions, we'd be fine—no, we'd be *happy*.

Buddha nature is at the heart of every living being? What about criminals? What about serial killers? Surely, I'm not saying that this applies even to them?

Actually, I am.

Eighteen years ago, I worked an odd freelance job. One of my brothers, an independent filmmaker, had been hired as a researcher for a movie called *Cape Fear*. When he had to go work on one of his own projects, he handed the job to me. Robert De Niro was preparing to play a psychopathic killer who seeks revenge on the lawyer who put him in prison. Part of my job was to write reports for him on a variety of nasty topics, from rape in prison to revenge to serial killing.

I had always avoided reading about serial killers; it creeped me out. When I got that job, though, I had no choice; I needed to examine a fundamental question: What makes a person become one? In movies and thrillers, the answer is usually taken for granted. The notion is that they're inhuman, walking personifications of formless evil. As I began my research, though, I discovered a very different reality. In the vast majority of cases that have been studied—ones in which the killers were identified and caught—it turned out that, as children, they had been severely physically and sexual abused, or received actual physical damage to the brain. Or both. In other words, they started out as innocent kids, and then suffered incredible trauma, and their minds were warped. (Obviously, everyone who suffers severe abuse doesn't become a killer, but that's one big element of this particular syndrome.) At the root of their vicious behavior I found incredible suffering, and a terribly sad, deluded wish to get rid of it by projecting it on others.

I think there's a general truth here. The world is full of bullies and sadists and people who do horrible things, but if you dig deep, I believe you'll find that they're really acting out of deep internal pain. I'm certainly not arguing that criminals don't deserve justice, yet every human being—no matter how deluded they might be—also deserves our compassion.

I don't mean to sound flippant, but if I could feel compassion for a serial killer, surely I could muster some for my ex-wife.

This business about everybody having an essential Buddha nature can make a big difference in the way we see other people. Normally, we often classify folks in terms of their jobs or outward status in life. *That's the dry cleaner,* we think. *That's the deli counter guy.* When we put people in those kinds of slots, it's easy to dismiss them. If, on the other hand, as you hand your money to the deli counter person, you think, *This is a fellow human being who wants the same things I do—and a potential Buddha,* you'll naturally treat him with more respect. Buddhists have a term for this more compassionate way of thinking: Equalizing Self With Others. As Shantideva puts it, "Because we are all equal in wanting to experience happiness and avoid suffering, I should cherish all beings as I do myself."

I think about this meditation when I eat in restaurants. I often see diners treating waiters as if they were serfs, barely worthy of acknowledgment or respect. That drives me nuts. I've worked as a waiter, and I know how hard the job is. That makes it easy for me to empathize—I can easily see myself in their place. I always try to make direct eye contact, and to speak with them as I would hope to be spoken to, and to tip well if I receive decent service. I don't see waiters as *waiters*—I see them as people like me, working hard to make a living, helping me to be well-fed and satisfied.

In a relationship, this way of looking at others can be very helpful. My friend Barbara explains how it has altered her view of her partner's behavior. "Because I'm so self-cherishing, everything she did seemed like a reflection on me. Now that that's easier to recognize, I tell myself, *Why is this about you?* I don't have to take it personally. It has nothing to do with her level of love for me. If she's going out with her friends, or if I get jealous because someone is paying attention to her, I have to say *I'm the same way. Every-body loves attention.* If I recognize that in me, I have to be okay with it in her."

When you take this notion a step further — a big step — it's called *Exchanging* Self With Others. The idea is to go beyond seeing other people as your equals, and to see them as *more important.* You exchange the object of your cherishing from yourself to them.

Such a radical shift cannot come easily. Another Buddhist meditation might help prepare the way. It's called On the Kindness of Others. When we think about it, it's clear that our comfort depends on the efforts of many other people. The clothes we wear were sewn by someone else, the food we eat was grown by someone else, the home we live in was probably built by others, the electricity we use was gener-ated by others, we can speak and write because we had teachers. We're alive thanks to the kindness of our parents, who took so much trouble to raise us. When we reflect on all that, it makes it easier to feel compassion for other people, and harder to treat them without respect.

Even so, compassion is often hard to generate.

Maybe part of the difficulty arises with the word itself. My dictionary starts by describing it as a kind of *sympathy,* and that in turn seems to imply *pity.* I smell a sense of conde-scension lurking in there, the notion that when we're com-passionate, we're standing outside someone else's experience, feeling sorry for them, looking down.

On the other hand, a selfless cherishing of others seems to imply looking up. It feels too austere to be possible.

When I sat on the subway looking at so many other sad or distracted or anxious people, though, I didn't feel above or below anyone. I felt like one of them.

Ultimately, it's not really a question of sacrificing yourself in order to serve others. That still sounds too severe. I was riding the subway yesterday, rereading *Everyday Zen: Love and Work* by Charlotte Joko Beck, and something she said really jumped out. "As we practice . . . , more and more we begin to turn away from a self-centered orientation—not to an 'other-centered' orientation (because it includes ourselves), but to a totally open orientation."

In other words, it's not about *me*.

It's not about *them*.

It's about *us*.

Earlier, I quoted Pema Chödrön saying that, "Instinctively I knew that annihilation of my old dependent, clinging self was the only way to go." This sounds scary, like we're being asked to abandon ourselves.

The thirteenth-century Sufi poet Jelaluddin Rumi offered a comforting perspective on this issue. Although we tend to think that merging with the greater world would make us feel like a drop of water lost in the ocean, he explained that we can look at it the opposite way: that the drop of water *takes in* the full glory of the sea.

And that's hardly a loss.

◁

So far, we've explored a number of Buddhist insights. To be honest, though, understanding them intellectually may not do a lot of practical good. To be able to act on them, to change our behavior, we have to *feel* them.

When we get to the third section of the book, I'm going to offer some specific techniques that may help you appreciate the insights in a deeper way. To show what I'm talking about, I'll give one example right now.

I've mentioned the soft-spoken Irish Buddhist nun whose talks I attended early on. Those sessions began with a half hour of group meditation. So there we were, a group of maybe forty New Yorkers, most of whom had come direct from day jobs, sitting in the pews of a Unitarian church, eyes closed. At first, our teacher encouraged us to calm and focus our minds by concentrating on something very simple and basic: the intake and exhalation of our breath. After we settled down a bit, she asked us to imagine that with every outbreath, we were expelling all our worries and anxieties of the day, like a stream of dark smoke. Then she asked us to imagine that with every inbreath we were taking in a blissful clear light.

One day, during a talk on compassion, she introduced a radically different version of this exercise. It was called Taking and Giving. Her soothing voice instructed us to think of someone with whom we were having great difficulties. (You won't be surprised to hear that I pictured my ex-wife.) I expected the teacher to instruct us to imagine that we were expelling our difficulties with every breath.

In fact, she did the opposite. "I want you to think of the suffering of this other person," she instructed. "Now I want you to breath *in* that suffering, as if you were taking *in* a stream of dark smoke."

The meditation continued. "And I want you, with every outbreath, to imagine that you are sending them a calm, blissful clear light."

This session took place just months after Claire left. I was agitated and angry with her, and the idea of taking in *her* problems certainly seemed counterintuitive—hardly something I was eager to do. As I tried the meditation, though, my anger drained away. I grew sorry for Claire—I could feel that she must be suffering too. I could hear the little girl in her saying *What about me?*, worried that she wouldn't be taken care of. I felt my love for her return, the love that was buried under my bitterness and resentment.

When I was angry, I found that there was no room in my heart for compassion. When I felt compassion, I found that there was no room for anger.

That good feeling lasted for a while after the session. It didn't make any difference to our relationship, because by that point I had little contact with my ex-wife, but I can imagine that under other circumstances it could have made a great difference for both of us. What if we shared custody of a child, and had to deal with each other in person several times a week? What if I did that meditation right before I had to see her? What if, instead of perceiving her as a mystifying, infuriating stranger, I was able to say: She's a fellow human being, suffering, just like me?

The positive change in those meetings might have been huge.

where have all the good friends gone?

If the houses stood separate, the damage might have brought grief to just one family, but they were connected, and so the fire leapt from one to the next, ravaging nearly a whole Brooklyn block.

Several minutes after it broke out, I got a panicked, tearful call from Anne, a friend who lived in the middle of the block. I rushed over and found her and her husband, my old friend Steve, penned behind a fire department barrier, distraught, as they watched smoke pour out of the burning homes. I stood with them all afternoon, and did my best to comfort them, and when a fire lieutenant finally allowed us to duck inside for five minutes, we waded in through several inches of sooty water and I helped them decide what to grab.

I was still married at that point; after their apartment was condemned, Anne and Steve stayed with Claire and me while I sent word to all my friends about this couple who desperately needed a new home.

A couple of years later, when my marriage fell apart, I learned that a divorce is like a fire in a row of houses: it starts with one couple, and then flares out through a whole connected world of family and friends.

Some of my friends were enormously kind and supportive — they invited me to dinner on a regular basis, called frequently to make sure I was okay — but others took the news oddly. Some just used my news as a springboard to talk about their own problems, or quickly changed the subject. For some, this evidence that a fairytale romance might not go "happily ever after" made them anxious about their own marriages. Some, I think, were simply made uneasy by someone else's suffering.

Naively, I didn't expect our mutual friends to feel that they had to take sides. After all, this was not some case of infidelity or abuse, where one party was obviously to blame. It was a matter of two adults who couldn't reconcile their different approaches to life.

Yet how did those friends react? One hung up when I answered the phone one night. (Thank you, Caller I.D.) Another, my wife's friend who had stayed in our home for several months while she was leaving her own husband, e-mailed to say that she couldn't offer me any support because she was "waiting for the dust to settle." I was shocked. I had made dinner for this woman, offered her many cups of tea, done my best to console her during her own time of trouble. Now she was waiting for the dust to settle!

The reaction of Anne and Steve stung most of all. Despite the fact that I had been friends with them for years before I met my wife, that they were now living in the apartment I had found for them, they didn't call to ask how I was doing. They didn't even drop me an e-mail — and how much effort does that take?

I wrote to say that I was saddened by their lack of support. Anne didn't answer. Steve e-mailed back to say that he was really busy, but perhaps we could do coffee next week?

I was flabbergasted, and so hurt that I literally began to lose sleep; I'd lie awake nights, straining to make sense of their behavior. Now, I had not helped them because I expected that it would be a *quid pro quo*, that I would deserve something in return farther down the line. Still, I couldn't begin to understand how they could have suffered so, yet care so little about my troubles. I felt as if they were treating me like a leper. Sometimes their indifference felt as painful as the divorce itself.

It went beyond the bounds of my understanding.

Or did it?

⌐

The human brain has an amazing capacity to "forget" or to deny.

Less than a year before, my wife's other best friend left her own marriage. I didn't know the couple very well, but the husband was a writer too and he and I had become friendly. They lived on the West Coast, so we didn't see Eric after his wife left him, but he began to call us frequently, leaving messages to ask why we had not said anything about their impending divorce.

Claire immediately took her best friend's side, even though she had also been very close with Eric. Out of what now seems to me like some strange and terrible laziness, I followed suit. While his wife seemed calm and rational, Eric had become like a wounded animal, flailing about and bellowing in his agony. That made my wife and me uncomfortable, and their breakup seemed to somehow point up a vague dissatisfaction in our own marriage. Taking sides was—above all—*easier;* it meant that we could avoid acknowledging the messiness and complexity of life.

It pains me now to say that we didn't return Eric's calls. After he left several more wild messages, I sent him a brief, platitudinous e-mail of sympathy, hoping that would get him off my back. It didn't; his messages became more pointed and accusatory. How could we have abandoned him? Didn't we care at all?

This next part makes me cringe. I finally sent Eric an e-mail saying that, though I was sorry about his troubles, I felt that he needed to learn to take his hard knocks like a grownup. "Your breakup is tragic," I wrote, "but it's not something that you need to be making the business of people all over the United States."

What comes around goes around.

Months later, in the midst of my own troubles, I sent Eric another e-mail. I told him that I didn't expect him to be able to forgive me for my callousness, but I wanted him to know that I finally understood what he had gone through. Though I had not done so voluntarily, I had been able to truly put myself in his place, and I experienced how the reaction (or nonreaction) of friends could add so much to the trauma of divorce.

"I see now," I wrote to him, "how little it costs to just offer a little human compassion and sympathy."

He wrote back to say that he was grateful for my letter and was willing to put the past behind us.

I was moved and humbled.

I wonder if I could be so forgiving.

Years later, I still struggle to come to grips with the way Anne and Steve and some of my other ex-friends behaved. I strain to be understanding. They must have felt caught in a complex situation, and been confused about how to act. I wish I could tell them what I've learned.

Believe it or not, I would say, the answer is not complicated or difficult. If you find yourself in a situation where two friends are getting divorced, simply treat them as you would wish to be treated. (In other words, trying putting yourself mentally in their place.) Don't let your fears or confusion cause you to remain silent or back away. Don't wait to be asked for help—that may well be interpreted as a lack of concern.

You don't have to make judgments or take sides. All you need to do is to offer sympathy, to check if both friends are okay, to let them know you're there if they need you. The point is so simple that it can be summed up in two little words: *be kind*.

Not long ago, an old friend of my wife's called for her. She was stunned when I gave her the different phone number.

"I'm so sorry to hear this sad news," she said. "I hope you're doing all right, under the circumstances." There was a pause, and then she added—refreshingly—"I'm sorry, but I don't know the right thing to say."

"Don't worry," I told her. "You just said it."

if you meet the buddha

At this point, I need to interrupt our discussion of the Buddhist path through divorce.

If you have studied Buddhism before—or even just heard about it through references on *The Simpsons*—you may have noticed that I've somehow managed to get far into a detailed discussion of the subject without ever mentioning the word *reincarnation*. And I've only referred to *karma* once. These may seem like staggering omissions, like offering a dissertation on astronomy without ever mentioning gravity.

For practitioners of the more traditionally oriented schools of Buddhism, both of those concepts are a big part of the picture. The current Dalai Lama, for example, is considered to be a reincarnation of previous Dalai Lamas. And karma is offered as a central explanation of how life works: it means that every action bears fruits directly in proportion to its nature. Do something good now, and you're planting the seeds for a good experience in the future. Do something unkind, and something unpleasant will eventually bounce back. The idea is not that certain actions are sins that must be punished (Buddhism doesn't really have a concept of *sin*); it's considered more like a simple, impartial law of physics: every action will result in a corresponding experience down the road.

To a certain extent, we can easily see the truth of this. If we generally do kind and generous acts, we'll receive obvious rewards: people will want to be around us, we'll probably have lots of friends, we'll often get help when we need it. On the other hand, if we're cruel and stingy, we'll suffer isolation and alienation.

The thing is, though, that karma doesn't seem to fully make sense unless it extends into past and future lives. We can turn on a TV any day and see unkind, stingy, and even criminal people who are rolling in money, fame, and material comforts. Likewise, kind and generous people suffer accidents, illness, and the most brutal tragedies. How can we explain that? Logically, it seems that only two answers are possible: either karma doesn't exist, or else it operates on a longer scale—people are being rewarded or penalized based on behavior in previous lives.

In other words, a belief in karma seems connected with a belief in reincarnation. And I'm not at all sure what to think about that. My teachers have been incredibly clear and convincing when making the case for so many elements of the Buddhist way, but I've noticed that when I ask for evidence that reincarnation exists, they tend to get a bit vague.

ʊ

One of the chief things that attracts me to Buddhism is that it never demands blind belief. The Buddha developed his teachings based on intensive personal questioning, contemplation, and analysis. He was a scientist working in the laboratory of his own mind, and he encouraged other people to make sure that they could replicate his findings.

He said that a teaching should only be accepted as true if one could personally determine that it is "skillful, blameless, praised by the wise, and conducive to well-being, prosperity, and happiness." He went even further, warning, "Do not be satisfied with hearsay, or with tradition, or with legendary lore, or with what has come down in your scriptures, or with conjecture, or with logical inference, or with weighing evidence, or with bias toward a view that has been pondered over, or with someone else's ability, or with the thought, 'The monk is our teacher.'"

I find that incredibly refreshing. Unlike so many spiritual leaders who seem defensive and intolerant of doubt, he wasn't saying that people would burn in hell if they didn't follow him, or that they should believe just because he said so. He said, in essence, *Here's what I have to offer. Check it out and see if it works for you.*

(Likewise, I encourage you to challenge every statement in this book. As we go along, ask yourself: Does this make sense to me, based on my personal experience? Can I test this for myself?)

Over and over again, I've been able to see the truth of the Buddha's ideas in action. I've gotten disappointed about something, and then recognized my desirous attachment. I've lashed out in anger, then probed inside and seen how it arose out of self-cherishing. But karma and reincarnation?

Not so easy to test.

Maybe I'm just a rookie, and the answers are waiting for me farther down the path, or maybe karma and reincarnation require a degree of faith that I'm not ready to accept. I'm not a Tibetan, raised from childhood to believe that these are obvious facts of life. (Plenty of Westerners seem perfectly willing to believe that they're going to die and fly up into the sky, rest on clouds, and play harps—or go down inside the earth and get taunted by a bearded devil with a forked tail. Why this should be any easier to accept than reincarnation might be the subject for another book.)

In any case, here I am, touting the benefits of Buddhism, yet questioning a couple of its major tenets. Where does that leave me? Am I just practicing a sort of convenient, bastardized Buddhism Lite?

Likewise, if you want to try out some of the ideas in this book, but are not interested in becoming a Buddhist yourself, would you be doing the same?

For an answer, we can turn to the Buddha himself.

At one point he was traveling through an Indian region called Kosala, inhabited by a group of people known as the Kalamas, and they approached him with some of their questions and doubts, including whether or not they should believe in karma and reincarnation.

The Buddha's answer was surprising. In an extraordinary talk called the Kalama Sutra (a *sutra* is a teaching), he told them, "Suppose there is no hereafter and there is no fruit, no result, of deeds done well or ill. Yet in this world, here and now, free from hatred, free from malice, safe and sound, and happy, I keep myself."

In other words, he was saying that even if he was utterly wrong about karma and reincarnation, the results of acting as if they exist would still be positive and beneficial. *Even if I'm wrong.* The more I think about the amount of religious intolerance, fear-mongering, and closed-mindedness in the world today, the more I admire this man.

When, in the middle of a talk given by the patient, good-humored Irish nun I mentioned earlier, I raised my hand and asked why I should accept the notions of karma and reincarnation if I couldn't easily test them, she didn't get upset, and she didn't say that I was deficient or wrong in my thinking. She simply asked me to keep an open mind, rather than rejecting the notions outright, and to be patient enough to explore them further.

It won't hurt me to learn more about karma and reincarnation before I make any judgments about whether I believe or not. And even if they don't exist, what's the worst that could happen if I pursue a Buddhist path? I might still end up a little more compassionate, generous, calm, and happy.

From the point of view of divorce, by the way, a belief in karma offers some interesting benefits. Instead of blaming our spouses for our suffering—and getting angry at them—karma suggests that our suffering is simply a result of our own past actions. (There's no one else to blame.) Likewise, instead of wailing *Why me?*, cursing at what seems like an unjust universe, and getting depressed, we can look at karma and see *this* is *why you.* At first blush, that might not seem so comforting, but seeing your own part in your troubles can lead to a greater acceptance of suffering, and make it easier to move on. Buddhism also offers the concept of *purification:* the idea that our present sufferings represent the flowering of the seeds of past actions, and that by experiencing them now, we're paying off a debt—instead of viewing suffering as a punishment, we can see it as a means of liberation from an unhappy cycle. Finally, karma means that we can control our destinies: if we don't like what we're experiencing now, we can change our behavior in order to get better results down the pike. If we behave with kindness and compassion, we're sowing the seeds for better future relationships.

Some traditional Buddhists would probably frown on the Western notion that we can custom-design our own practice, picking and choosing from the elements that make sense to us. On the other hand, Buddhism doesn't seem to be either/or: either you accept all of its doctrine, or you can't benefit from any of it. Buddhist sages have likened the teachings to a diamond. Unlike many objects, which have little value if you break them into smaller pieces—like a teacup, for example—they say that the teachings retain value even if you only accept a part of them. (You're still left with a smaller diamond.)

From the very start, the Buddha established a tradition of personal questioning of his teachings, an insistence that you *have to* come to your own understanding. Zen Buddhists express this in a startling way: they say, *If you meet the Buddha on the road, kill him.* This isn't some kind of weird incitement to violence; it means that if you believe that the teachings are something *out there* (like happiness), then you're on the wrong path. Like many other initially puzzling Zen statements, it's meant to shock us out of smugness, blind observance, and attachment to an ossified set of beliefs. It reminds us that Buddhism should be a deeply personal, internal quest.

In his book *Buddhism Without Beliefs*, which argues that it's possible to pursue an entirely secular Buddhist path, writer Stephen Batchelor puts it this way: "While 'Buddhism' suggests another belief system, 'dharma practice' suggests a course of action. The four ennobling truths are not propositions to believe; they are challenges to act."

If you're interested in Buddhism, you have to find your own path. You need to go with what feels right to you.

A few months ago, I attended a Buddhist festival for the first time. I was amused to find that it took place in a legendary Jewish resort hotel in the Catskills. ("Ladies and Gentlemen, appearing tonight in the Starlight Lounge: Lama Shecky!") I rented a car, drove up on a beautiful fall day, and found myself in a hotel lobby swarming with lay attendees from all over the globe, who were dressed in the casual trekkers' attire you might find in a youth hostel, and bald-headed Buddhist monks and nuns decked out in wine-red and orange-yellow robes.

The people were friendly and warm, but I hardly knew anyone. I attended the talks and meditation sessions, and they were interesting, but I felt left out as the attendees, many of whom knew each other from previous festivals, chatted and socialized in the hallways. I began to feel isolated. What happens next in such times? I became depressed.

There I was, already feeling out of the general swim of things, and then I went to an evening session: a big auditorium filled with Buddhists from around the world. As I've noted, I'm not big on ritual and liturgy. To my dismay, this session turned out to be strictly a prayer hour, accented by various rituals (bowings, offerings, etc.). To make matters worse, the prayers had been set to modern music. Now, I wouldn't have objected to hymns accompanied by glorious music by Johann Sebastian Bach, or rousing gospel music. I might not even have minded traditional Buddhist monastic chanting (which sounds, frankly, a bit like the croaking of bullfrogs.) But no—these were childlike, sing-songy melodies, accompanied by acoustic guitar and flute. The songwriter in me was offended; I was reminded of the sixties movement to add guitars to Christian services and "make them relevant to the young people."

I glanced around and saw several thousand other people singing along enthusiastically, quite unburdened by my aesthetic complaints, but I was miserable. Where were the brilliant insights? Where was the practical advice? This was not what I had signed on for. I considered leaving earlier than I had originally planned.

But then something interesting happened. The festival was staffed entirely by volunteers. I knew the woman in charge of running the snack-time café. *What the hell*, I thought—*I might as well sign on for a few shifts. At least it'll give me something to do between sessions.* I spent some time behind a bar, handing over bottles of spring water and soda. And then I worked the payment table, taking cash from people and making change. I began to chat with strangers. I joked with my fellow volunteers. I had fun. And then it hit me. Okay, maybe the praying and singing was not my cup of tea. But when I volunteered to help other people—when I stopped worrying about whether the occasion met my needs—I relaxed and enjoyed myself.

I almost laughed. I couldn't have asked for a more perfect Buddhist lesson.

I've been known to wax rhapsodic about Buddhist insights, and I know that there's a bit of the fervor of the new convert here.

When people ask me if I'm a Buddhist, though, I tend to answer that I've begun *practicing* it. That's an important distinction. Buddhism is not about taking on some fixed identity; it's about learning how to behave in more positive ways. Saying "I'm a Buddhist" is just giving someone else an opportunity to add a file in some rigid mental category and to make judgments. (Buddhists themselves are not always exempt from such powerful identification, unfortunately, nor immune from some petty rivalries between various schools and leaders.)

The Buddha himself discouraged overidentification with his own doctrine. He described it as a raft to get to the other shore, the end of suffering. He said that once you cross over, you wouldn't bother to carry the raft around.

This morning I read something that put such identification in an even more surprising perspective. (Here it is again, that delightful shock of Buddhist insight, like a blast of wasabi that makes you feel like the top of your head has just been lifted off.)

In his book *Turning the Mind Into an Ally,* Sakyong Mipham, Chögyam Trungpa's son and a profound thinker in his own right, has this to say: "When he began to teach, the Buddha was just reporting his observations: 'This is what I see about how things are.' . . . He wasn't preaching dogma; he was pointing out reality. Saying that impermanence is a Buddhist belief is like saying that Buddhists believe that water is wet. The Buddha didn't create impermanence or selflessness, suffering or peace; the Buddha just saw reality, noticed how it works, and acknowledged it for the rest of us."

I love that. It's so easy to get caught up in worrying about religion — *What institutions do I identify with? Am I following the doctrine to the letter?* — that before we know it, we're more concerned with labels than with the deeper reality they're trying to describe.

Water is wet. Self-cherishing and anger are destructive. You don't have to be a Buddhist to see that.

The Dalai Lama himself is tolerant of many different types of belief, including other religions. In fact, he reaches beyond belief to recognize that someone can commit positive actions without any religious doctrine at all. And he summarizes his own faith in this profoundly simple, powerful, and all-inclusive way: "My religion is kindness."

raccoons

Back on my own path, I was gearing up to sit down at my computer when the desire rose into my mind for a snack. It was a lot easier to face the refrigerator than a blank page, so I succumbed. (I had an itch; I was gonna scratch it. The never-ending search for happiness . . .)

I entered the kitchen. Before I even got to the fridge, I was stopped by a bizarre cacophony, coming from the ceiling. Harsh scrapings, loud clunkings, weird chatterings. If I had heard these noises just after I moved in, I might have been tempted to attribute them to an unhappy ghost. When I first noticed them, I thought my upstairs neighbor's cat was going crazy trying to reach a mouse. I quickly reconsidered; it couldn't be the cat, unless the beast had doubled in size and started mainlining catnip.

Finally one night, the mystery was solved: my neighbor looked out his kitchen window and saw four raccoons marching single file in the moonlight. Somehow, the creatures had managed to gain entry to our roof, and now they were burrowing into the crawlspaces between the ceilings and floors. One day, my neighbor was about to get into his shower when he looked up next to a water pipe and saw a big *paw* scrabbling down through the ceiling. We called the City info line and were told that Animal Services only deals with domestic animals like dogs and cats. The operator suggested that we buy or rent some traps. *Then what,* we wondered? What were we supposed to do with four yowling, very unhappy raccoons? Take them to the park?

I did some Internet research and found a product that was supposed to repel them, a spray containing coyote urine. (Seriously.) We hadn't gotten around to ordering it yet, so now I was standing in the kitchen listening to the creatures scrabble away. Some primordial feelings arose in me. First of all, fear. What if these wild creatures managed to break through the sheetrock and tumble down into my apartment? What if they had rabies? The fear morphed into anger. *If I had a pellet gun,* I muttered, *I'd bust a cap in your little raccoon ass!* (I wouldn't really do that—not very Buddhist and all—but growling back at the ceiling seemed to make me feel better.)

Sounds like a true external problem, right? Soon I was going to have to do something about this home invasion, and I was definitely not gonna be able to *meditate* the critters out of the house.

In the meantime, though, I had found an excellent object for some Buddhist contemplation. What interested me was the way I had managed to create a firm sense in my mind of the inherent nature of the raccoons: that they were marauding, malicious creatures, determined to interfere in my life.

If I stepped back, though, and strove to be more objective, I could easily see how distorted this image was. From the raccoons' side of things, they were just animals seeking shelter from the elements. *Hey, guys—if we burrow a little here, we can get into this nice warm, dry space!* (Like me, they were striving to be happy and to escape suffering.) They were hardly out to get me. In fact, they were probably barely aware that I even existed.

From my side, my image of the raccoons was greatly influenced by their proximity to me. If I saw a picture of a raccoon in a nature magazine, I might just say, *Aw, look, what a cute little guy!* If I saw one on someone else's roof, I might just be amused. *(A raccoon! In Brooklyn!)* But here they were, invading *my* space, and I was getting all emotional about it.

I was not seeing the raccoons as they were—I saw them as they affected my own cherished self.

If you think about it, we see most animals this way. We view kittens and puppies as inherently cute, sharks and grizzly bears as inherently menacing. . . . I imagine that this sort of stereotyping is a protective evolutionary trait; we've learned to view nature in terms of its potential impact on *us*.

Unfortunately, we also do the same thing with other people. We separate them into categories based on their relationships with us: friends, enemies, loved ones, strangers. . . .

The raccoons have brought us face to face with the trickiest, most difficult-to-grasp concept in all of Buddhism. It's called *emptiness*.

The Buddha said that our root delusion is ignorance. It has two components. The first is self-cherishing, our wrong tendency to see ourselves as the most important thing in the universe.

Now we've come to the second part. It's called *self-grasping*. This doesn't just refer to grasping at our sense of self—it means that we wrongly believe in the inherent nature of *everything*. We grasp at the notion that things exist in the way that they appear to us.

In truth, Buddhists believe, nothing in the universe has an essential, fixed nature or reality. Not raccoons, not sharks, not friends or enemies. *Nothing*. Not even inanimate objects.

As Matthew pointed out when he held up that book in my first Buddhist talk, we look at it and see *book*, whereas a tribesman from the Amazon might look at it and see only *mysterious object made of pressed-together white leaves*. Or we point up at a bunch of stars and say, *Big Dipper*. Does the Big Dipper exist anywhere but in our own minds?

The point is certainly not that everything doesn't exist, or that it's all meaningless and illusory and morally equivalent. It's that we need to be aware that the meaning and value are coming from *us*. As Geshe Kelsang Gyatso says, "If we were asked which was more precious, a diamond or a bone, we would say a diamond. This is because a diamond is more useful to us. However, for a dog a bone would be more precious because he can eat a bone whereas he cannot do anything with a diamond. This indicates that preciousness is not an intrinsic quality of an object but depends on an individual's needs and wishes."

As with all things Buddhist, the most important fact is not that things happen to us; it's that we give them meaning by filtering them through our minds. I heard an amazing true story the other day that provided a unique demonstration.

On October 24, 2004, an obscure independent rock band from Vermont drove down to New York to play a club gig on a Sunday night, a lousy time for any rock 'n' roll show. Three normal paying customers showed up.

As the band took the stage, though, thirty-five more people suddenly poured into the club. What the band didn't know was that a group of New York pranksters who specialized in staging fake public events had chosen this particular show for their latest gag. The "agents" who made up the unexpected crowd had been given copies of the band's CD in advance, so they knew the words to every song. They had been instructed to behave as if they were diehard fans, and they even wore homemade band T-shirts and fake tattoos. When the musicians began to play, they shouted their approval, sang along, and danced wildly. The band was baffled by their sudden popularity, but they responded by playing their very best. After the show ended, all of the pranksters quickly left the club, without explaining anything. On the long ride home in their van, sweaty and tired, the musicians mused about what had turned out to be one of the best gigs—and nights—of their lives.

It didn't take long, thanks to the Internet, for them to learn that they had been the subjects of a very clever practical joke. Ira Glass, of the National Public Radio show "This American Life," subsequently interviewed the band, and I was particularly struck by what the guitar player had to say. He related how, as a kid, he had always felt like a nerd, and was taunted by his classmates. Becoming a member of a band had finally given him some hope that he might gain more social acceptance. At first, during the New York gig and for a few hours after, it seemed as if his dream had miraculously come true. And then, when he learned about the prank, he became hugely depressed. It was, he said, as if his worst nightmare had been realized. Once again, he had been made a butt of fun, only this time people all over the country were laughing at him.

The story, which at first seemed hilarious, had taken a tragic turn—but it didn't end there. The guitar player concluded by saying that he had thought things over some more, and that eventually he felt a huge sense of relief. Something he had feared greatly all his life had actually happened, and he had found that he could survive it. Ultimately, he was left with a profound sense of freedom and release. (As an added bonus, his obscure band was written up in *Rolling Stone*.)

Notice that the physical event never changed, but the guitar player went through three very different ways of looking at it: one of the best nights of his life; one of the worst experiences of his life; a great opportunity for personal growth.

Did that strange concert have any inherently existent meaning?

Evidently not.

⊡

Okay, you may be saying to yourself at this point—well and good, but what about Buddhism and *divorce?* As it turns out, this idea of emptiness has huge implications for relationships.

To use an example closer to home, Claire began to see me as an inherently angry person.

If that were true, then everybody I come into contact with would perceive me that way. In fact, some of my friends and acquaintances have *never* seen me get angry. Tina, my ski-tripping date, said that I seemed like such a mellow person that she couldn't even *imagine* me angry. Likewise, some people I work with see me as a serious, hardworking person; they'd be shocked to learn that my close friends see me as someone with a goofy sense of humor, or that in my mid-twenties I was the lead singer and guitarist for a loud, fast rock 'n' roll band.

Angry, industrious, goofy, rockin'—do I have one fixed identity? Claire started to react as if I did. I'm sure I did the same thing to her. Unfortunately, we both began to tell ourselves rigid stories about what kind of person our spouse was. He's *an angry person.* She *always* does x.

Ironically, we even tell such stories about ourselves. We might say, "I'm a shy person," or "I'm a lazy person," or "I'm a person who doesn't like strange foods." And then we limit what we can be or do. For the first thirty years of my life, I saw myself as a bookish nonathlete. I truly believed that this was my nature. (I would have been shocked to see my older self running around the park, or practicing wild kung fu moves.)

Just as raccoons or bones or constellations don't have an inherently fixed identity, neither do *we.* The great irony, ultimately, is that we spend so much time cherishing and protecting a self that isn't really there.

We tell ourselves stories, and they take on such weight and power that they can determine our reality. I recall an axiom from a college sociology class: *If we perceive something as real, it can have real consequences.* Here's the example the professor used: if we believe that goblins are lurking along a certain path in the woods, we might take a different path. The goblins are imaginary, but our idea that they're there affects our real actions.

We do this all the time, in all sorts of ways.

We hold endless beliefs about how the world works, about what other people are like, about our own identities. And we act on those beliefs every day, every hour. Sometimes this false sense of fixed identities has trivial consequences. If we believe that we're not good at eating strange foods and so we resist trying octopus, there's not much harm done. Sometimes, though, our stories about who we are, and who other people are, can cause serious damage—as in a marriage.

Once we decide that our spouse has a certain identity, or that we do, that perception can become very hard to change. I'm reminded of a French-Canadian movie called *Leolo*. One of the main characters, a scrawny kid, gets regularly beaten up by another kid in a local alley. The victim goes away, spends several years working out, and transforms himself into a muscle-bound weightlifter. Then he returns to the alley, site of so many adolescent humiliations, and finds the bully, now half his size. We're sure we're about to witness a satisfying scene of retribution, but something surprising happens. The bully doesn't back down. He reaches up and shoves his old victim in his massive chest. And our hero *crumples.* Yes, he managed to make over his outer self, but inside, he's still telling himself the same old story.

Due to her personal history, Claire learned to tell herself that she was unable to tolerate conflict or anger, that she was an extremely sensitive, fragile person. Actually, she's one of the strongest-willed people I know. (Before I met her, she spent two summers alone in that Arizona mountaintop fire lookout, hauling water and supplies, driving a very dangerous road, braving lightning storms and utter solitude.) When problems cropped up in our marriage, though, she reverted to that old sense of her vulnerable, precarious self—and her actions followed from that limiting view. And I brought my own sorry personal baggage to the affair.

Becoming conscious of the myths we cling to about our partners and ourselves won't miraculously enable us to revolutionize our behavior. Old stories die hard, and we've had a lifetime to train ourselves to view the world and ourselves in rigid ways.

But if we can become more aware, to realize that we might need to shake up our belief in what we "know"—to be able to see that a raccoon is just looking for shelter, or that our "angry" spouse is really just threatened or afraid—that's a big start.

the heart of the matter

Returning once again to our subway parable, we usually see the gum-poppers as inherently problematic. Adopting Buddhist tools, we can change our perception and choose to see them as opportunities. The catch, though, is that they're *neither.* Both perceptions are coming only from us. Someone else sitting next to a gum-popper might be thinking, *This person has excellent taste in shoes,* or, *This person is sexy.* However we perceive the stranger, none of those qualities are actually coming from their own side. If they were, everyone would see them the same way.

Instead, we always see the world through the lens of our mind, with all its preconceptions, prejudices, and expectations. We create meanings, and then imagine that they're coming to us from outside. As the old adage puts it, *We see the world not as it is, but as we are.*

I think of that whenever I hear someone say, *I could never have children because I don't want to bring them into a world like this,* or complain about how the whole planet is going to hell. Of course there are reasons why life may seem bad now, from wars all over the globe to the steady destruction of our environment. But are things really getting worse? I read recently that just a couple of hundred years ago the great majority of humanity was living under the yoke of some form of slavery. Yes, the twentieth century was a bloodthirsty one, but there are reasons for hope: improvements in civil rights (in some countries, at least), medical advances, greater world communication through the Internet and other means. . . .

Maybe whether we're optimistic or pessimistic says more about *us* than about global conditions. And maybe our degree of happiness is based on our outlook on life, rather than on what events may happen to us. (Of course, that's the opposite of the way we usually think of things.)

A landmark 1978 scientific study put this question of where happiness lies to the test. Three social psychologists (Brickman, Coates, and Janoff-Bulman) looked at people who had won a lottery and people who had been rendered paraplegic in accidents. The researchers interviewed the subjects shortly after the events that radically altered their lives, and then again a year later.

In the first interviews, the lottery winners were predictably ecstatic, and the accident victims predictably glum. If those events had an inherent nature and meaning, that would make perfect sense: injuries would have to make us sad, and money falling from the sky would inevitably make us happy.

After a year, though, the study found that the impact of the events had faded considerably; in fact, both groups reported that they felt a substantially similar degree of happiness to what they felt *before* their "good" or "bad" fortune. In other words, their sense of well-being or suffering was not really founded in what had happened to them. Some scientists have suggested that this might be due to some sort of genetic happiness "set-point," but I suspect a different answer: that their sense of happiness was determined by their *view*.

This point is crucial; we're getting to the heart of the matter of where our happiness and suffering are really coming from.

An external event happens. In reaction, we experience a feeling. We think: *The event caused the feeling.*

Granted, there's a type of incident that strikes us in a very primal part of our brain—the limbic system, to be precise—and causes an almost immediate surge of emotion. If a tiger jumps out at us, we're likely to be flooded with fear, or a fierce impulse to fight. Most of the time, though, as Buddhism makes very clear, we fail to notice an essential middle step in the story. We're not reacting to the event—we're reacting to the way we view it in our own mind. The next time you feel an emotion, stop and dig deep into what's really behind it.

You'll most likely find that the feeling was prompted by a *thought*.

The usual thought is: *How well does this external event jibe with my expectations of the way life should be?* If it fulfills or exceeds those expectations, I'll tend to feel happy. When my wishes are not met, I'll get frustrated, angry, or sad.

Let's say you're recently divorced, and you didn't make a social plan for the weekend, and Saturday night rolls around and you find yourself home alone. You start feeling lonely, and then sad. Is the fact that you're at home by yourself inherently depressing? Not at all. If you had loud and messy visitors from out of town overstaying their welcome with you for a full week, and they finally left, you'd be delighted to be alone. So why are you sad now? Because you're thinking: *It's Saturday night when I'm supposed to be having fun doing something social, and other people — people in relationships, or the kind of people I see on TV shows, or the celebrities I see in magazines — are probably doing something glamorous, out on the town, and what's wrong with me that I'm home, and not at some fun party?*

See what I mean? These are all *thoughts* about the meaning of the situation. They're based on a *view: Saturday nights are for parties, and happiness comes from going to parties, and I'm not at a party, so I have a reason to be unhappy.*

So what do you do?

You seek out a party.

And what happens?

Maybe you have a blast. Or maybe you get all excited about dressing up and going out, and then you get there, and the crowd is different than you expected, or you're not crazy about the music, or people don't seem very friendly. Just as you can be quite content when you're alone, you can be lonely in the middle of a party. You've experienced that, right? Again, the problem isn't the party. It's your view that parties are a guaranteed source of happiness.

When I was doing high-end, high-society catering, I often worked inside the homes of very rich and famous people. One client was a multibillionaire, and I often wondered why he kept hustling to make more money. I mean, if you've got a billion dollars, you've pretty much guaranteed yourself every possible material comfort. Would he even be able to tell the difference between having one and two billion dollars?

Again, it comes down to *view*. The guy believed that money would guarantee him happiness, and it couldn't, so he had to keep chasing after more. He would *never* have enough.

As Sakyong Mipham puts it,

> If we don't know how to be content in our mind, we can't even be content with our food. Eating at the best restaurants in the world won't make any difference. There is someone in a village in India eating curry out of a clay bowl, more content than we are. When we find the pair of shoes we want, for a brief moment we feel content. But when that moment passes, we're on the move again: food doesn't taste good, clothes don't fit, the sheets are too rough, the bath's not hot enough. We need better movies, more exciting books, a new relationship. We need to live on a different planet.
>
> Desire is a creature with an endless appetite. Like a spark put to dry grass, it just consumes. By its very nature, it can never be satisfied, because it is rooted in the aggression of looking outside ourselves for relief. That expectation always results in disappointment, self-generated pain. It's the mind giving itself a hard time.

So what's the way out of this trap?

First of all, when we feel angry or sad or jealous or impoverished, we can learn to recognize the thoughts—the view—that lies behind those feelings.

I'm depressed about my marriage. Why? Because my spouse is not meeting my expectation that marriage should be a program for making me happy.

Then we can see how we try to alter reality to meet our view.

I try to change my spouse's behavior, so that he or she will do the things that make me happy, and stop doing the things that make me unhappy.

We're embarked on a huge project, not just in our relationships but in our lives in general. We struggle to make more money, to get different jobs, to find praise and recognition—we try to change our external circumstances. It's a tough, constant, and very frustrating battle. As Shantideva noted, to protect ourselves from stepping on thorns we can't possibly cover the entire world with leather.

But—he wisely added—we *can* cover our own feet.

In other words, there's a much simpler route toward happiness than changing our entire world. We can start on the other end of equation: we can learn to change our view.

I once laughed out loud when I saw this sign in a diner: "If our restaurant doesn't meet your expectations, please lower your expectations."

The point here is not that you have to lower your expectations, necessarily, but that you can learn to be happy from your own side, whether life presents you with four-star restaurant meals, or simple bowls of curry.

It all starts in your mind.

This may well sound too simplistic. Surely there are events that necessarily provoke certain feelings?

Let's say you're strolling down the street and a stranger suddenly walks up and punches you in the face. You're gonna get angry, plain and simple. Not even a buddha could say that this was an opportunity to experience happiness.

Actually, though . . . anger seems like the only reasonable response here, but you could broaden your options if you had a different view.

Let's say you realized that the person who threw the punch must have necessarily been suffering in some way to do such a stupid thing. Let's say you felt some compassion for them, and asked them what was wrong. Let's say they broke down and told you that they had just had a fight with their spouse. (Remember the guy in the real estate broker's office?) Let's say you were able to talk with them about it, and help them calm down. Maybe you could help them see that throwing wild punches at strangers would only exacerbate their problems. Maybe, after practicing patience and compassion in this way, you might even start to feel happy.

Maybe not. Let's say that the person refused to calm down. Let's say they hit you again, and you ended up having to go to the hospital. No possible cause for happiness there, right? But who knows? Maybe you'd meet your future spouse in the emergency waiting room.

We don't know how things will turn out.

One of the most famous Zen stories concerns a farmer who owned a fine horse. One day, the horse escaped from its corral and ran away. "What terrible misfortune!" the neighbors cried. The farmer just shrugged and said, "What's good, what's bad? Who knows?" The next day, the horse returned, accompanied by three strong wild horses. "What incredible good fortune!" the neighbors cried. The farmer shrugged. "What's good, what's bad? Who knows?" The next day, the farmer's son tried to ride one of the wild horses and broke his leg. "What terrible misfortune!" the neighbors cried. The farmer shrugged. "What's good, what's bad? Who knows?" The next day, the emperor announced that all able-bodied sons would have to go off and fight in his latest war. "What incredible fortune, your son's broken leg!" exclaimed the neighbors. The farmer shrugged. "What's good, what's bad? Who knows?"

That farmer was able to live with a light heart, because he wasn't continually rocked by external events.

This is the great bonus of emptiness: when we hear the word, we tend to think of a hole, of a lack, of something negative, but emptiness is actually full of options. When we see that things or events don't have a narrow, prescribed meaning, we find that our range of possible responses (and feelings) expands enormously.

Emptiness leads to *freedom*.

Two years ago, if you had asked me how I felt about the end of my marriage, I would have seen it as nothing other than a cause for anger, depression, and grief.

If it had not happened, though, I would probably never have seized the opportunity to learn more about Buddhism, and to write this book.

And when I think that this book might help someone else who's going through a rough time, I feel *happy*.

beginner's mind

And now we return to the story about Tina and her ski trip.

You'll remember that I left several voice messages for her, and went into a tailspin when she didn't call me back. Instead of just letting myself sit with my confusion about what was going on, instead of accepting my groundlessness and lack of control over her behavior, I rushed to fill that void by jumping to conclusions.

She's rude and inconsiderate. She doesn't really like me. She met a ski instructor.

Luckily, because of my new Buddhist training, I didn't let those imaginings lead me to express my frustration. I was able to pause and think, to open myself to a broader range of possibilities.

Japanese Buddhist master Shunryu Suzuki was once asked to summarize the essence of Zen. I love the way he encapsulated it in one short phrase: *not necessarily so.* Stay open. Don't approach the world with a set of expectations and beliefs and preconceptions. See every moment fresh. He called this essential approach to life "beginner's mind."

One of our biggest problems is that, instead of maintaining this wide-open mind, we tend to interpret everything in relation to our cherished selves. As a writer, for example, I have to show my work to other people on a regular basis. If I ask a friend to look over a manuscript and don't hear back soon, I tend to jump to the worst possible conclusion, which always relates to me: *She hates my piece, and can't bring herself to say so.* Then I'll learn that her lack of a quick response had nothing to do with me or my writing—that she was simply out of town, or dealing with a family crisis. I'm working on getting better at dealing with the inevitable waiting time, better at simply accepting the not-knowing and lack of control.

Not necessarily so. It all comes back to Matthew's example of the gum-popper on the subway. Without the openness of beginner's mind, we look at him and decide, *Uh oh, a problem for me.* We never get to the point of *Aha! An opportunity to practice patience,* not to mention being able to see the transgressor as a person in his own right.

Due to my new exposure to Buddhist thought, I tried to take a wider view in my new dating life. Instead of lugging all my past baggage to each situation, I tried to see things fresh. Instead of trying to figure out where a relationship might be headed, I did my best to slow down and look at what was happening right now.

It occurred to me that maybe Tina's phone silence was not a rejection of me—that, in fact, it wasn't about *me* at all. Maybe she was just having her own hard time post-divorce. Maybe she was just as excited as I was about our sudden new passion, but maybe that excitement carried an under-current of anxiety and stirred up unresolved feelings about her own ex-spouse.

When she got back, I went to see her. Instead of smooching it up right away—kissing, after all, can be a way of avoiding speech—I raised the issue of why she had taken so long to call me back. She confided that she *was* nervous. I told her that I felt the same way.

And *then* we lay down on the couch and brought each other some joy.

If you were to ask me what advice I would give for improving a relationship, I might start with this: don't assume that you know what your partner is thinking or feeling. You can see their actions, but not the thoughts behind them. Don't jump to interpret those actions in terms of how they appear to you, of how they relate to your cherished self. Work on taking a wider, more compassionate, more open view—you might well be surprised.

Maybe you think your wife is acting out of selfishness, but she's really acting out of fear that her needs will be ig-nored. Maybe you think your husband is acting out of an angry nature, but he's really struggling to protect an inner wound.

Why is this open-mindedness so important? Because one little misunderstanding can start off a big chain reaction. The next step might be a sense of being wronged, which leads to a feeling of hurt, which leads to anger, which leads to a fight or some other harmful action. If you frequently jump to conclusions, you're likely to fall into the vicious spiral of miscommunication and distrust that Bill Ferguson warned about, the one that results in both partners pulling away from each other until there's no common ground left.

Ferguson suggests a positive and incredibly simple way to escape this syndrome fueled by ignorance:

"Stop talking and listen."

lighting the loop

Let me not to the marriage of true minds
Admit impediments. Love is not love
Which alters when it alteration finds,
Or bends with the remover to remove:
O no; it is an ever-fixed mark,
That looks on tempests, and is never shaken . . .
—WILLIAM SHAKESPEARE, "Sonnet 116"

My ex-wife is a fan of Shakespeare's sonnets. Evidently, she didn't take Number 116 very much to heart. When she found some alteration in me—or at least when the me she saw didn't match her mental image of what I *should* be—she tossed the *we* of our marriage overboard and set sail in the other direction. She decided that her new goal was simply to minimize her own suffering.

I didn't do much better. Looking back on things, I see that my love was deeply shaken when she behaved in ways that didn't match my wishes. In terribly stupid ways, I blinded myself to that "ever-fixed mark."

Last week I went to a concert that featured some beautiful piano music by a composer named Enrique Granados. During the intermission, I noticed this program note: "Granados died young: the ship he was traveling in was torpedoed by a German submarine and sank. Although he managed to reach a lifeboat, he saw his wife drowning and jumped back into the sea. They both died."

When I think of their selfless love, I'm moved—and ashamed.

◁

Matthew, my first Buddhist teacher, put my shaky version of love in context in a talk the other night. "There's an uncertainty in our relationships because they're contingent and conditional. It's very difficult to get along with people if our view is that our good relationship is contingent on them behaving in a way we like. This view is foolish because it doesn't produce the results we're looking for—and yet we cling to it. People appear to be behaving inappropriately or unpleasantly, so we think, *They are unpleasant*. We want to get rid of people who don't 'behave.'"

Matthew capped his talk with one of those radical, counterintuitive Buddhist zingers that have so often stopped me in my tracks.

"We think people are loveable or unloveable depending on how they behave. No—they're loveable *because we love them*."

◁

The radical message of Buddhism is that the world is not something *out there* that we can only react to. It exists for us in our own minds, and we have the power to change our minds. If we learn this lesson in a deep way, the impact on our loves and friendships can be huge.

I spoke of a good relationship as a loop that glows. We know how a negative charge can destroy that loop. We perceive our partner as behaving in an unpleasant way; we get defensive or angry; then they perceive *us* as unpleasant; *they* react in a negative way; and things rapidly go to hell in a handbasket. It's like the saying about computer programming: garbage in, garbage out. We put negative energy in, and get negative energy back. If we think that we're just reacting to what our partner does, then it's impossible to change that equation.

But if we see that, like everything else, the loop exists within our own minds, we can make a revolutionary change: we can pump positive energy in, and charge the loop so that it lights up like an amusement park's great Ferris wheel at night.

I'm thinking of an article I read in the *New Yorker* recently. I don't watch the TV show *24*, but the article pointed out that it often endorses the use of torture as a way to get suspected terrorists to spill their guts. The writer interviewed some of the world's foremost experts on interrogation (including some very hardcore military vets), who testified that in real life torture rarely produces the desired results. That's especially true of fundamentalist fanatics such as members of Al Qaeda. If Americans torture them, it only reinforces their view that Americans are evil, and boosts their determination to clam up.

The interrogators consistently found that the best way to get information from suspects was to treat them with respect and consideration, to acknowledge them as fellow human beings. That dazzled the captives. They expected to be tortured and abused by the Great American Devils—to have their sense of our inherently evil identity confirmed. When they were treated in a radically different way, that made it hard for them to hold onto their fixed negative views. Eventually, they often opened up.

Imagine if we could startle our spouses that way. Obviously, my example is extreme, but if you want to heal a difficult phase in your relationship with your spouse or your ex, try doing the opposite of what they expect. If you're sinking into a downward spiral, if your partner is starting to see you as a problem and an obstacle, the next time they do something that bothers you, *don't fight back.* Surprise them with kindness and understanding. Instead of lashing out in defensive anger, of falling into that *you always do that* trap, shake things up by doing something loving. Instead of arguing, shut up and listen. At the very least, you'll break out of a repetitive, stale, and unproductive cycle. And you might get some very positive results.

◻

The *New York Times* runs a regular column about relationships called "Modern Love." One recent column, by a writer named Amy Sutherland, made quite a splash. While researching a book about a school for exotic animal trainers, Sutherland found that trainers have two opposite styles. Some work by punishing unwanted behavior: they might withhold food until they get the desired response, or even physically wallop their trainees. Other trainers *never* use negative techniques; they get results solely through positive reinforcement. (They ignore unwanted behavior, but are quick to reward any actions that lead in the desired direction.)

Meanwhile, at home, Sutherland was growing increasingly frustrated with certain aspects of her husband's behavior: he left his dirty socks lying around, he interrupted her while she was busy, he got in a bad mood every time he lost his keys, which happened often. "I used to take his faults personally," she wrote. "His dirty clothes on the floor were an affront, a symbol of how he didn't care enough about me." (Self-cherishing, anyone?) She tried to improve him by nagging, to little effect, and she grew increasingly resentful and frustrated. Finally, it occurred to her that she might try applying the positive animal training techniques she was learning about at the school. When her husband did something she didn't like, instead of responding with anger or sarcasm she just ignored it. When he did something she *did* appreciate, like picking up his socks, she offered praise. "At the school," she wrote, "I'd be scribbling notes on how to walk an emu or have a wolf accept you as a pack member, but I'd be thinking, 'I can't wait to try this on Scott.'"

This may sound rather crude and manipulative. I'm not encouraging you to think of your spouse as an animal to be trained. But there's an important lesson here. Instead of demanding that her husband change, Sutherland made a conscious decision to change her own behavior. Instead of nagging, she pumped positive energy into the loop of their marriage. And her efforts paid off. Her husband gradually stopped doing the things that bothered her, and their relationship improved.

I was reminded of the above story by a Buddhist talk I went to last night. The subject was friendship. The teacher pointed out how we tend to divide other people into three categories: friends and loved ones, people we're neutral about, and enemies. We think we're making these distinctions based on inherent qualities in these people; that they're *likeable*, say, or *unpleasant*. The Buddhist approach, unsurprisingly, is very different. The idea is not just that we can learn to "put up with" people who rub us the wrong way — it's that we can actively increase the number of friends in our life and decrease the number of enemies by thinking about people differently. The teacher, a young, very cheerful Buddhist monk, talked about learning to *enjoy* other people. "You can make friends with everyone in your mind, from your side. You can become *a friend of the world.*"

That phrase reminds me of a friend of mine, an amazing man named Sunny. He's older, with long gray hair and a noble face. He goes by his nickname, and he earned it. He's a painter, but he earns his living as the owner of a bar, an old waterfront Brooklyn saloon. I vividly remember the first time I went there. Many bars on a busy Saturday night have an unpredictable, jittery feel, fueled by alcohol and testosterone, but this was the opposite. Sunny seemed like an incredibly affable, cheerful guy, and his spirit set the tone for the entire establishment. The next time I went back, Sunny welcomed me as if I was an old, long-lost friend. Upon repeated visits, I noticed that he greeted *everyone* that way. He smiled a lot, and people lit up when they were around him; they wanted to bathe in his bighearted company.

When I feel unsociable or petty or distant from other people, I try to think of Sunny's radiant example. He *enjoys* people, and they enjoy him back. He transforms the world around him.

⊙

Earlier, I mentioned that I could walk into a party and immediately start making judgments about who I was attracted to. Obviously, that's all about self-cherishing, and the results weren't so great. Maybe I didn't see anyone who appealed to me on a sexual or romantic level, or maybe I did and got rebuffed. Every now and then I'd have a happier experience, but the odds didn't seem to be in my favor.

After studying Buddhism, I can see that I often treat life in general like one of those parties. That narrow view doesn't lead to a very high rate of success in the happiness sweepstakes.

The next time I walk into a party, I'm going to try a little experiment. Instead of narrowing my focus to people I'm attracted to, instead of judging the evening based on whether I find them and they seem to like me, I'm going to try to see every single person I meet as someone worth talking to. I'm going to try acting friendly and kind, instead of waiting for other people to treat me a certain way. Instead of focusing on my own happiness, I'm going to see if I can't cheer a few other people up. If I have some good interactions with people, if I have some interesting conversations, if I can enjoy the company of people I might have previously ignored, I'm going to consider the evening a success.

If I can learn to walk into life that way, maybe I'll be better prepared to walk into another marriage.

all things go

After I was forced to leave my old apartment, I panicked about ending up in a dingy basement studio. Instead, I found myself in an airy, light-filled apartment in a leafy green neighborhood, with a front porch, a deluxe double-sided re-frigerator/freezer, even a chandelier. And my new back patio was an unexpected bonus, balm for my troubled mind. I could sit out there and read, and look up into the trees, and enjoy the changing light as the sun moved across the sky.

One morning I looked out the glass sliding door and saw a brick lying on the patio tiles. I was baffled. I went out and looked around, toward the street, toward my neighbors' yards. Had someone thrown it over my fence? If so, why? I stood there, mystified—until I turned around and looked up. The chimney above my new home was tilted at a precarious angle. And several bricks were missing from the top. I won-dered if the whole thing might come crashing down.

I began to notice other problems with the house. When it rained hard, water poured in through a leak over the kitchen's sliding door, and also in my bedroom closet. Plumbing problems started to crop up, and my upstairs neighbors and I had to call for emergency repairs. Then the raccoons came.

At any other time, I would undoubtedly have become anxious and upset about these problems. But I had just survived the worst period of my life. So many things had changed, as if a tornado had spun through: my wife was gone, my apartment of sixteen years had been sold out from under me, my familiar neighborhood had been priced out of reach.

I didn't freak out about the household surprises. I was fed up with living on an emotional roller coaster.

And life was teaching me a powerful Buddhist lesson.

I got the same message another way. Alone in my unfamiliar new apartment, I began to crave fresh air and exercise. I decided to dedicate some time every afternoon for a run around nearby Prospect Park. I started jogging in the fall, when the dense greenery of summer was giving way to clouds of red and orange and yellow—and then the leaves began to fall. I bought some rather embarrassing running tights, and ran on through the winter, too, as the trees went bare and sightlines opened up, revealing the hidden contours of the landscape. I ran on as the crowds faded away, and I would complete the three-and-a-half-mile circuit with only a few other hardy souls for company. The regular exercise boosted my mood considerably, and the exposure to nature helped me get out of my own gloomy, self-cherishing little head. And it helped me to see that the world has been operating in one obvious way forever.

Everything changes.

We tend to believe that life is relatively stable, and then every once in a while a change comes along. We're drastically mistaken. *Everything is already changing, all the time.* The weather constantly shifts. Plants grow or wither. Our clothes wear out. Businesses start up and fail. Buildings are built, buildings are torn down. Cells in your body are constantly dying and being replaced. On physical, emotional, and intellectual levels, you're literally not the same person you were just five minutes ago.

I think of the afternoon when Claire and I stood out on that Brooklyn pier, reciting our wedding vows. Whoever wrote them certainly recognized life's inevitable state of flux. "For better, for worse; for richer, for poorer; in sickness and in health . . ." That's a very wise pledge.

The problem comes with the last line: "Till death do us part." Even now, though I think of Claire less often, I still have moments, when I'm in the middle of crossing a street, perhaps, or drifting off to sleep, and suddenly I'm hit with a pang of profound loss. I had a very close bond with a woman I loved, I thought that we had a fixed future together, and it's still hard to believe that they're both completely gone.

That *thought* leads to great sadness. If you're going through a divorce right now, I bet you often feel sad too.

When we hold on to the ways things used to be, the way we want them to remain, we suffer. We're ignoring the evidence we see around us every single day. This is the way life goes: *everything that arises eventually falls away.* Buddhists have a word for this fundamental fact: *impermanence.*

Two days before I moved into my new apartment, a hurricane tore into the Gulf Coast of the United States, breaching levees and flooding the city of New Orleans. Overnight, what had for centuries been one of the country's most distinctive, best-loved cities was nearly wiped out. Like most Americans, I could hardly believe it. I don't mean to imply that my divorce pain was on a par with the sufferings of the victims of Hurricane Katrina. (As Humphrey Bogart once said, my problems didn't amount to a hill of beans.) But the root principle was the same: *everything that arises eventually falls away.*

We all live in houses (our bodies) that lose parts and need repairs. We get sick; we grow old. And there's a chimney waiting to fall on each and every one of us. Instead of repressing or denying it, Buddhism encourages us to meditate directly on the inevitable fact of our own death. That may sound depressing as hell, but it can free us from a lot of anxiety. The simple fact is that, whether we like it or not, change is all around us, and death is on the way. That's absolutely normal—we're the ones who are adding all the drama and fear. Change and death just *are;* there's no point in fighting them. As the thirteenth-century Zen teacher and philosopher Dogen beautifully put it, "A flower falls, even though we love it; and a weed grows, even though we do not love it."

I had a flash of insight about this last summer as I was on my daily run through the park. I came to a little lagoon which branches off a larger lake, and stopped to take in the view. It's a calendar-picturesque spot, with an arching stone bridge over the water, graceful willow trees, and a white boathouse that resembles an elegant Italian villa. That week, though, the lagoon had become covered with a thick scum of pea-green algae. I remember thinking, *This view would be so great, if only that algae wasn't there.* And then, because I'd been reflecting on some teachings, I realized my folly. The algae *was* there, and all the *if onlys* in the world wouldn't change that fact. I laughed at myself, and then I accepted the view in front of me, and then I jogged on.

If we don't want to accept change, we cling to things, they change anyhow, and we suffer. If we *do* accept it, we can learn to live with a much lighter heart.

And don't forget to look at impermanence this way as well: it doesn't mean that all situations go bad. If you find yourself in a tough spot, that's likely to change too, often for the better.

◖

As I went deeper into Buddhism, like the farmer in the parable about the horse, I found myself less rocked by external events. As a freelance writer, for example, I had been tremendously dependent on what agents or editors might say about my work. Rejections left me anxious and depressed. Now, I worry less about things I can't control.

Some events, like hurricanes or terrorist attacks, certainly seem like they're all bad, and it may sound callous to suggest otherwise. Years after 9/11, though, the *New York Times* caught up with many of the victims' surviving spouses and families, and their stories were often deeply inspiring. Many had taken their tragedy as a wake-up call, and given up meaningless jobs for new careers. Many had improved their relationships with their surviving loved ones.

When loss comes, it helps to consider what we still have. I'm grateful that I'm alive, that I'm healthy, that I live in one of the world's most affluent societies and have the time,

opportunity, and freedom to think about spiritual growth —
a luxury many people don't have because they're too busy
scrambling to be able to eat. (When I start feeling depressed
about my writer's "poverty," I can go on the Internet to
Globalrichlist.com, enter my annual income, and find that I
make more money than 90 percent of the people on the
planet.)

We all have a great deal to be thankful for.

Instead of getting depressed by talk of suffering and impermanence, I've found that practicing Buddhism has given me
a lighter, more adaptable feeling about life.

I think of a famous retired basketball player whose daughter asked him how he could tolerate listening to an arena full
of booing fans. "I didn't listen to the cheers," he replied.
"Why should I worry about the boos?" He realized that he
couldn't control the audience's fickle response. Instead, he
focused on his own enjoyment of the game. No matter what
was going on up in the stands, he found his happiness inside.

We can all do the same. We can't stop change, or control
our spouses, or inoculate ourselves against everything that
might happen to us in life. *And we don't have to.* It has been a
big relief to let go of some of my attachment to the idea that
things always have to go my way. I don't freak out every
time some new glitch springs up in my apartment. I know
that this place is not mine forever, and that I could be out on
the street again tomorrow. As a result, I don't cling to it. I'm
hugely grateful for whatever time I have in it, as I'm grateful for my time in this body, and for the happy times with
Claire.

If I do worry about losing my home, if I start falling back into the old notion that I need a certain kind of external setting in order to be happy, I think of Buddhist monks who were taken from their monasteries and spent decades imprisoned in tiny cells in Chinese prisons, subject to isolation, abuse, and physical torture. By every standard we hold dear, they had every reason to suffer. (Certainly, far more reason than some divorced schmo.)

And yet they could remain tranquil and at peace.

It makes you think, no?

Excuse me, I'm getting a little fired up here. The last thing I want is to start sounding like one of those cheerful zombies on a TV infomercial. ("I've tried the Abdominalizer in my home, and it really, really works!")

The fact is, though, that Buddhism *has* worked for me. I'm still just a rookie at being able to apply it, and I still screw up on pretty much a daily basis, but I can say with some confidence that I'm as happy now as I was before my marriage underwent a drastic change.

Most of the time.

part three

ARROWS INTO FLOWERS

chops

It was a brutally hot, muggy New York day. I was exhausted from a hard freelance job the day before. Now my brother was giving me a ride to a family gathering, and he was late, as usual. I often get a bit edgy before such get-togethers, and I was grouchy before I even got in the car. To make matters worse, my brother was blasting his car stereo.

I told him to turn it down.

He told me to "chill out."

Anger flared up within me. (Odd, isn't it, how the people we love the most can press our buttons so easily?) "Stop the car!" I shouted.

Before it had even come to a halt, I was halfway out.

"Well," my brother called after me, "I guess your *Buddhism* is really working out. . . . "

At the time, that comment got me even more steamed, but now I can look back on the incident and laugh.

My brother was right, of course. I had spent more than a year studying the harmful effects of anger, I knew how it worked, I even knew something about how to prevent it — and there I was, totally losing my cool. All those talks, all those books, all that meditating . . . *poof.*

On the other hand, my brother was wrong. A year is a very short time when you're trying to change your whole way of life. Of course I hadn't miraculously become some enlightened being, impervious to insult and injury. Geshe Kelsang Gyatso gives a three-step recipe for getting rid of such delusions as anger: *Recognize, Reduce, Abandon.* Sometimes, it was all I could do just to recognize the folly of my behavior.

As the above story should make clear, though, recognizing the problem is not enough. The challenge is to *act* better. Buddhism can be a huge help in repairing a damaged relationship, or recovering from a failed one, because it offers very specific, practical advice about what to *do.* It's all about learning to move through life more skillfully.

What's our goal? A vivid allegory provides a great answer. After years of spiritual seeking and struggle, the Buddha decided that he was going to go sit under a bodhi tree, and he resolved that he would not get up until he had attained complete awakening. While he sat there, a powerful demon called Mara came by, backed up by an army of fearful monsters. They drew their bows and shot a storm of arrows, hoping to distract the Buddha and frustrate his quest. But he was in such a deep state of peace and calm that he just sat there, and watched as all the approaching arrows transformed into flowers.

What a fantastic metaphor for our struggle through divorce! Wouldn't it be great if we could do the same? What if we could stop our spouse's barbs from wounding us? And what if we could send kindness to our partner, instead of arrows of our own?

When you're having an argument with your ex, though, that compassionate intention is liable to fly right out the window, and the next thing you know you're in the middle of a shouting match.

Fortunately, Buddhism offers more than just awareness of the ways in which ignorance and anger and desirous attachment get us in trouble. It suggests antidotes to those poisons. The antidote for the suffering caused by anger, for example, is the practice of patience. The antidote for self-cherishing is the practice of compassion. The antidote for selfishness is the practice of generosity. The antidote for jealousy is to practice rejoicing in the good fortune of others.

Antidotes don't work unless we apply them, and we have to train in how to do that. Again, the key word is *practice*. Musicians call it having *chops*. Knowledge of music theory didn't allow me to jump up on stage and play guitar solos. I had to get familiar with the instrument. Like any skill, that required effort, discipline, and repetition. The ability to play the notes had to be ingrained into my nervous system until—ultimately—it became second nature.

Anger is a particularly demanding emotion. Trying to remain calm in the middle of an interaction with an ex-spouse often requires the virtuosity of an accomplished classical musician. How the hell can you practice *that?*

You can break it down into smaller steps. The first is to realize that anger is always harmful. The second is to develop a wish to get rid of it. The third is to make the effort to learn where it comes from—your own mind—and what causes it to arise: a sense of injury to your cherished self. Through meditation, you can gain some control over your mental agitation.

And you can familiarize yourself with the antidote (patience) by trying it out on lots of small irritations: slow-moving traffic, a long line at the post office. . . . Hopefully, when you need to have a discussion with your ex, you'll have gained the skillfulness to go into it with a calmer mind—you'll be more able to stop those feelings of anger from even arising.

Simple, right?

Unfortunately, no. It takes real focus and effort. But that's better than the alternative: the suffering caused by all of those poisoned arrows.

○

At times, my divorce brought out the worst in me. I went on a campaign to prove to my spouse that she was wrong. I often felt that I might feel better if she felt bad.

These days, I think of an amazing Buddhist concept called Accepting Defeat and Offering the Victory. Says Geshe Kelsang Gyatso: "Having gained some experience of love and compassion for others, now we need to put this good heart into practice in our daily life. For instance, when someone out of anger or jealousy harms or insults us, with our mind abiding in love and compassion, we should happily accept the harm and not retaliate."

Happily accept the harm. Wow.

When someone shoots arrows at us, we don't have to shoot back.

I'm reminded of tai chi, where I learned that I didn't have to meet oncoming force with any resistance. I could just smoothly step aside.

I wish I had been smart enough to practice that while I was still married.

Luckily for her, my friend Barbara has the wisdom to put this great advice into practice now, when she finds herself in the midst of a fight with her girlfriend.

"Arguing," she says, "is not a skillful way to come to some kind of resolution. Anger and jealousy are not solutions to what we're fighting over. The word 'relationship' means *relating,* and if we're arguing, we're not relating."

She probes deeply into her desire to argue. "Where does it come from, this opposing force? Does it make my experience more real and solid if I have a strong view that has to be right?" Thanks to her exposure to Buddhist thought, she has learned to be less dogmatic — she recognizes that her sense of righteousness is not necessarily based on reality.

She adds that, "The phrase *according to the level of delusion* has become very important to me. After three years of practice, I still act according to my level of delusion. And I have to allow my partner to be at her level of delusion, and to be more accepting of that."

This strikes me as an excellent aid for reducing anger and increasing forgiveness in relationships. I think back to things that Claire did as we approached our breakup, things that seemed hurtful or threatening to me at the time, and I can say to myself, *She was doing the best she could, according to her level of delusion.* I think back to things *I* did that I regret, and I can cut myself a little slack. *I was doing the best I could, given my own level of delusion.* (As with forgiveness, the point here is not to allow an evasion of responsibility, or to excuse harmful actions — it's simply to increase a spacious feeling of understanding and compassion.)

Barbara does her best to transform disagreements with her partner. "Even though I still get angry and we still have fights, I'm looking more at her end. Now, even if I think she's dead wrong, I see that she believes it in her heart—that's her experience of it. And if I'm stuck in a view, I have to look at her and say, *She feels exactly the same way—that* I'm *stuck.* I think, *What's a skillful way to help her understand?* Equalizing Self With Others is about bringing down the enemy wall. It's *I know how you feel,* not *I want to prove my point.*"

During tough times, Barbara remembers the ultimate goal of being in a relationship. "The Dalai Lama says that love is about two people in a state of mutual respect trying to en-hance each other's happiness. I've been able to let go of my need to put up an opposing force. If we're fighting and I know that [my girlfriend] really believes something, I'll offer the victory to defuse the situation. It's more skillful than fighting with her. If you have a *must win* attitude, you're get-ting the other person angry. If you offer the victory, it stops that on both sides.

"Now I think, *If she really wants to win the argument, why can't I give her that?* It causes her happiness."

And Barbara tries to keep her own fears and self-cherishing out of the picture. "I try to think, *Forget about me getting hurt—how can I help my partner?*"

I'm inspired by Barbara's efforts to apply her new aware-ness to improving her relationship. She recognizes, though, that she's engaged in a long-term project. "It's a work in progress," she says, smiling. And she makes me smile when she says that her style of practice involves "jumping in, gradually."

sitting

Don't just do something, sit there.
— VIETNAMESE BUDDHIST MONK THICH NHAT HANH

As I hope I've made very clear by this point, Buddhism is not about blissing out and ignoring life; it's about becoming *more* aware. It says that the first thing we can do to increase our happiness, and the happiness of others, is to become *mindful.* If we notice that we're getting angry, we can do something about it. If we notice that we're thinking about ourselves to the detriment of others, we can knock that off. We can see how we're becoming overly attached to things or to people, and abandon that harmful way of thinking.

Buddhism offers a very specific means to reach that goal: we can *meditate.*

189

By Western standards, sitting down quietly for a certain period every day may seem like a strange solution to life's problems, but people around the globe have been finding it helpful for thousands of years. Meditation offers many possible benefits.

Since we're talking about marriage and divorce, one of the most obvious things it can do is calm an agitated mind. If you're angry, it can serve as a kind of time out, a way to "count to ten" and avoid regrettable actions. Simply put, if you're sitting down by yourself in peace and silence, you're not shouting at your partner or otherwise screwing up your relationship with them.

Meditation is also a stress reliever. A difficult relationship can be literally nerve-wracking, as the body ends up contorted by tensions in the mind. During the last several months with Claire, I suffered back and shoulder pain so intense that I could hardly sleep. After my marriage ended, all those deep muscular knots "miraculously" disappeared. If you're still in the midst of conflict, scientific studies have shown that meditation can relieve backaches and headaches, lower blood pressure and cholesterol, provide relief from insomnia, and even boost your immune system.

You don't need any special equipment to meditate, and you don't have to pay a dime. The instructions are simple. You can start by sitting for just five minutes a day, or you can try a slightly longer period, like fifteen or twenty minutes. You can sit on cushions on the floor, or you can sit in a chair. You can close your eyes completely, or you can keep them half-open and directed at a low point a few feet away from you; either way, you should keep your back straight and perpendicular to the floor and your chin slightly tucked in. If you can, breathe through your nose, keeping your mouth shut, with your tongue pressed lightly against your upper palate (this saves you from salivating and having to continually swallow). Don't worry about trying to breathe in any special rhythm; just let the breath come and go naturally, filling and leaving your abdomen (rather than staying up in your chest).

Meditation comes in a number of different forms. The first is *placement* meditation. After you take a minute or two to check that your whole body is nice and relaxed, focus on something basic and stable, such as the passage of air in and out of your nose. The challenge seems simple: stay in the present; focus only on your breathing.

(That may seem like a dull exercise. In his book *Breath By Breath: The Liberating Practice of Insight Meditation,* veteran teacher Larry Rosenberg offers a unique response. "One new meditator kept coming to interviews with a chronic lament, 'The breath is so *bor*ing.' Finally I asked him if he'd ever heard of Brooklyn yoga. He said no. I told him to close his mouth tight and close off both nostrils with his fingers. We sat that way for some time until, finally, he let go of his nose and gasped for air. 'Was that breath boring?' I said.")

Like most beginning meditators, I found the practice very challenging. Within thirty seconds of sitting down, I noticed how not-calm my mind really was; it was like a zippy fish, darting this way and that. And when I meditated, it became shockingly obvious how little time I spent in the present moment. I regretted or waxed nostalgic for things that had happened in the past, was wishful or worried about things that might happen in the future. Whole stretches of time went by where I completely forgot that I was in a chair in my apartment; I flew off on mental tangents, envisioning future scenarios (what I wanted for dinner, what I should do on

Friday night . . .). Suddenly, I would snap to, as if I had dropped back onto the cushion from a jaunt into outer space.

For a rookie, that skitteriness of thought was disconcerting. Enlightenment seemed far away when I couldn't even focus on my breathing for ten consecutive cycles. Experienced meditators say not to worry. Distracting thoughts will inevitably arise, and that doesn't mean you're screwing up. The point, at first, is not really to avoid all thoughts; it's to become more aware of them, to see how they spring up, to realize that you can let them go. One way to do this is to notice when a new thought appears, to say (inwardly) *"Thinking"*—without any judgment about how well you're meditating—and then gently return your focus to the breath.

The thoughts and feelings that arise in the middle of a divorce are so powerful that they often feel overwhelming, but we can discover that they don't have to be so compelling. Gradually, we can learn to see that—like everything else in life—they're *impermanent:* they rise up, fill our minds for a while, then drift away. We can discover that we don't have to be swayed by each passing thought. As Rosenberg puts it: "Picture a tree in a powerful storm, with high winds and heavy rain. The tree is blown back and forth by the wind, often looking as if it will blow over, but it doesn't, because it has deep roots. In our practice, the deep roots are a stable sitting posture—that's what acquiring a seat is all about, developing composure and stability—and the storm can be a powerful emotion, like fear or loneliness or anger. . . . Once you have [developed stability], you can be with whatever storm comes up; you can really experience your emotions, which is the key to becoming free of them."

Another thing that meditation helps us realize is that we expend a great deal of mental energy in a totally useless exercise: *worrying*. We anxiously spin out all sorts of anxiety-producing imaginary scenarios, but unless we're really planning how to solve problems, all that agitation doesn't help anything. When I get a little hyper about some "problem," I reflect on this pearl of Buddhist wisdom, courtesy of Shantideva:

> If a problem can be solved, then there is no need to worry about it.
> If a problem cannot be solved, then there is no use to worry about it.

(Either way, you don't have to worry.)

In divorce, we're also liable to spend a lot of time brooding on the past. A famous Zen story addresses that tendency. A young monk and his master came upon a young woman hoping to cross a river. Despite the monastic prohibition against touching women, the older monk promptly lifted the woman onto his back and carried her across. As the two monks continued on their journey, the younger one fretted about this violation for hours. Finally, he told his master of his agitation. The older monk's reply was swift and firm: "I set that woman down at the other side of the river. Why are you still carrying her around?"

Learning how to see behind the false power of thoughts and feelings can start in a tiny way. I noticed in meditation that I might feel a small physical itch; for example, my nose might tickle. Normally, I would have reached up to scratch it, but following the principle of stillness, I just sat. What happened? I saw that this feeling that seemed to demand a response soon faded away on its own.

That's a neat little lesson of how we can resist knee-jerk reactions, a lesson that expands if we look at it in a bigger context. As Rosenberg puts it, "You grab the person who makes you feel good, kill the one who makes you feel bad. All of the areas that give human beings problems—sex, money, power, drugs, ethnic strife, war—have their source in feelings. The Buddha saw feelings as the weak link in this chain. If we catch them at their source, if we can skillfully see them, we can liberate ourselves from unnecessary suffering. We can short-circuit a process that leads to all kinds of human misery."

Western culture tends to see thoughts and feelings as coming from two different places, the head and the heart. We sometimes have a bias against thoughts, as if they're just thin and abstract, and believe that feelings are more genuine. We say, *Trust your heart.*

Remember back in Chapter One, when I was describing my apartment search and how I broke down on a city sidewalk? I didn't tell you the whole story. At that moment, even as I was flooded with emotion, I noticed that a part of me seemed to be standing apart, coolly observing my behavior. *So,* that inner watcher said, as if storing up the experience so I could write about it later, *this is what it feels like to hit rock bottom.* And then I berated myself, disgusted: *Can't you ever just let go and have a goddamn authentic feeling?*

The next summer, I happened to have dinner with a clinical psychologist and I mentioned this little episode. (I wasn't angling for free advice; we were discussing Buddhism and psychotherapy.) She reassured me that my split awareness was not some kind of abnormality. In fact, she pointed out, this kind of *superego* awareness is essential to human civilization. She had worked on psych wards for violent patients and noted that it's the people who *don't* have this awareness whom you have to worry about. (People who dissociate so severely from a sense of conscience used to be called socio- or psychopaths; now we say that they have *antisocial personality disorder.*)

It occurred to me that maybe I had things backward. I thought my grief was authentic and my mental observation of it somehow bogus, but maybe I had actually been experiencing a moment of Buddhist insight on that brutally hot city street. Even in my dire state, I was somehow aware that the emotion flooding my mind wasn't the same as my mind. It was just a cloud passing through. Such thoughts can swell into tempests, but if you have ever taken an airplane trip, you know that you can rise above a turbulent storm into a clear blue sky. Even in our darkest hours, that clear mind is always there behind the clouds, calm and stable.

Keep that in mind the next time a blast of feeling leaves you shaken. As Geshe Kelsang Gyatso wisely puts it, "Just as there is room in the sky for a thunderstorm, so there is room in the vast space of our mind for a few unpleasant feelings; and just as a storm has no power to destroy the sky, unpleasant feelings have no power to destroy our mind."

transform your *brain*

Thus far in meditation, we've been trying to focus on some single point, such as the breath. The goal is to calm the mind and to see that thoughts are just transient. To use another analogy from nature, we can picture them as waves. In a difficult relationship, especially a divorce, we can feel as if we're bobbing helplessly, tossed about. We get distracted by the waves and think that they *are* our mind — until we realize that even the biggest surges are nothing compared to the deep, still ocean below. Meditation can put us back in touch with the stability that's always available underneath. It takes a lot of practice to get good at it, but even a few minutes of sitting can calm that choppy water.

The next type of meditation is *analytical,* and it has two main forms.

First, you can meditate on a concept, such as impermanence or self-cherishing. The point is not just to figure these things out intellectually, in an abstract way — it's to gain a deeper, more *felt* experience of them. A good tip here is to meditate on ideas in a very concrete fashion. You could spend a year thinking about the general fact that self-cherishing is something to avoid, but that might not have much impact. Make it personal. Think about a specific incident with a specific person. Think—for example—about how upset you got when your ex was five minutes late picking up the kids, even though you were not really in a rush. Did your level of irritation match the actual inconvenience? Was she doing it to bug you, or simply busy with other things? Why did you take it so personally? Life offers no shortage of moments to analyze in this way.

When you feel like erupting into a spat with your spouse or your ex, meditate on the fact that they're essentially like you: they just want to be happy and avoid suffering. You can see that behavior that seems hurtful to you really arises out of their own pain. Go beyond abstract notions of happiness and suffering: try to genuinely see yourself in your spouse's place.

Sometimes a news story or photo has the power to jolt us out of our usual self-centered orientation and to connect us with the hearts of others in a primal, direct way. The story of Wesley Autrey and his subway rescue did that for me, as did the story of Victoria Ruvolo and the frozen turkey. I also think of a recent image by photojournalist Nina Berman. On the right of the photo stands a man in a Marine's dress uniform. The picture is shocking: the man looks like his face has essentially melted off. (While he was on duty in Iraq, a suicide bomber blew himself up nearby.) The image is so distressing that normally I might have shut down to it, shunting the soldier off into some extreme category of *other*ness—but then I looked at the left side of the picture, and saw his young hometown sweetheart standing next to him in a white dress. It was their wedding day. All the distance, all the otherness disappeared. My heart flew out to both of them in a way that went beyond concepts and words—I could begin to feel how intensely both of them had suffered, and see that all they wanted was to find happiness. Just like me. Just like all of us.

The saying *There but for the grace of God go I* has often seem odd to me. I know it's supposed to encourage compassion, but when I hear it I can't help thinking, *What about the other person? Are their sufferings also due to the grace of God? Are they really so different from me?* The challenge is not to see other people as like you if only the circumstances were different— it's to see them as like you *right now.*

At a moment when you're feeling a lot of tension with your ex, try viewing the situation through their eyes. Maybe you'll see that they're behaving just as you would if you were in their shoes. Maybe they're not the storybook villain you've built them up as in your mind—maybe they're just a person like you: scared like you, selfish like you, mean and kind and intolerant and generous and unforgiving and angry and capable of love, *just like you.*

◁

We have already moved into the second phase of analytical meditation: once your mind is more stable and your insight has deepened, you can use meditation to actively cultivate new mental attitudes. You can let your anger go, for example, and replace it with compassion.

Personally, I have found the meditation on taking and giving—the one in which you imagine yourself drawing in your partner's suffering as black smoke, and you breathe clear light toward them — to be the most effective way to break out of my own loops of bitterness and resentment. This isn't just some abstract mental exercise. Remember earlier how I mentioned that studies by social scientists have shown that acting out anger by punching a pillow can have bad neurological consequences — that it can actually strengthen the brain's pathways for anger? The good news is that the opposite is also true: it now appears that we can strengthen the brain's physical pathways for patience and compassion.

For hundreds of years the scientific establishment has viewed the brain as a pretty fixed object. Conventional wisdom said that its structures have roles that are determined from birth, and that its neural networks can't change or grow much after childhood. The last decade, though, has seen radical changes in the way neuroscientists have come to view the brain. As Sharon Begley points out in her book *Train Your Mind, Change Your Brain,* an exciting new body of research has shown that this three-pound gray lump has a major degree of *neuroplasticity* — that it's surprisingly flexible and adaptable.

One researcher, for example, studied people who became blind after birth. Scientists had long assumed that the visual cortex in such people would become dormant and useless. But new techniques of imaging electrical activity offered startling results: the subjects were shown to be processing *aural* information in the visual cortex. That is, they were processing *sounds* through neurons that were supposedly only useful for sight. In other words, a part of their brains had changed function in response to their life experience.

From a Buddhist point of view, though, the most crucial finding has been that the brain can physically change in response to *inner* experience—that is, in response to *thought.*

You already know that you can respond to a powerful external event with inner physiological changes. Let's say you narrowly miss getting hit by a car: your body floods with adrenalin and a scanner would show electrical stimulation in areas of your brain such as the limbic system. What's interesting here is that new tests have shown that your body and brain can show similar stimulation even if you just *imagine* getting hit by a car.

In other words, your thoughts can affect your body and brain. And that can be very good news. Let's say, for example, that you're depressed. Recently, psychiatry has fervently promoted the idea that biochemical malfunctions in the brain give rise to depressing thoughts. The solution? Alter the chemistry by taking pills. Meditation offers a radically different approach: you can improve your brain chemistry by learning to train your mind.

Buddhists have played an important role in this new research. Since 1987, some of the world's leading scientists have been traveling to Dharamsala, India, for a yearly Mind and Life Conference with the Dalai Lama and a group of Tibetan monks. Since he was a child, the spiritual leader has been keenly interested in Western science. Instead of seeing it as a possible threat to his own beliefs, he's fascinated by the ways in which Buddhism and Western science complement each other. He has encouraged fellow practitioners with tens of thousands of hours of meditation experience to submit to EEGs, PET scans, and fMRIs. These investigations have dramatically demonstrated the powers of the mind. And they have begun to offer firm scientific evidence of the benefits of Buddhist practice.

Psychiatry and psychology have long focused on treating mental pathologies, such as depression or anxiety. Buddhism also attempts to reduce mental suffering, but then it goes on to target a much more positive goal: developing actual *happiness*. It's easy to say that happiness should come from within, but that can sound a bit fuzzy and greeting-card-ish. Yet Western science is starting to catch up to what Buddhists have long been saying: that we can actually train ourselves to experience more joy.

During a recent talk, Matthew offered an interesting demonstration. While we sat for the initial meditation, he asked everyone in the class to bring to mind an enjoyable moment. I remembered a recent afternoon when I sat in my backyard gazing up into a cherry tree, a cloud of radiant pink blossoms.

Our tendency, of course, was to associate the joy with the external cause—*cherry tree=pleasure*—but then Matthew moved us away from that outer object. "Let the specific memory fade out in your mind," he said, "but hold onto the feeling." The fact that I could continue to bask in the emotion indicated that the pleasure was not in the cherry tree—it was being provided by my mind. In other words, the mind is capable of *creating* happiness. Experienced meditators, Matthew went on to say, can learn to call up happiness without having to go through the step of recalling any happy image—they have become familiar with that inner association of thought and feeling, and can bring it forth without any external influence at all. (Without lottery winnings, without new shoes, even without ice cream.) It makes perfect sense: if happiness exists only in our minds, why can't we learn to generate it by using our mental abilities?

Veteran meditators can generate compassion too. Even inexperienced meditators can do it. When scientists conducted a test of willingness to help a stranger, they gave one group of (non-Buddhist) subjects some mental *priming*—they asked them to think of people who had been kind and helpful to them in the past. That mental recall electrically stimulated areas devoted to compassion in the brain—and that group of test subjects actually gave more help to the stranger.

In short, like athletes in training, we can use meditation to prepare us to do good.

◁

From a traditional Buddhist standpoint, one of the biggest events we're training for is our own death. Serious practitioners lay the groundwork for that moment, so that when it comes—rather than being fearful and confused—they might be calm and free of anxiety.

This may sound silly in comparison, but I feel like I'm training for another future occasion. I haven't seen my ex-wife for almost two years. The strange thing about New York—though it's a city of eight million people—is that you tend to bump into people you know all the time. I'm sure that one of these days I'm going to turn a corner, or walk down into the subway . . . and there she'll be.

I try to anticipate how I'll behave. I imagine that I'll feel a powerful jolt of adrenalin, a heart surge of pain and anger and even love. And then what? Will I just walk on by without a word, or will I manage a civil Hello? Will I say something angry and unkind, or will I be able to show some compassion and concern?

To be honest, I don't know. I hope I'll manage to keep breathing calmly, and to call on the kindness I can summon toward her when I'm sitting on my cushion. On this point, Western neuroscientists and Buddhist spiritual masters seem to agree: by meditating on a potential meeting now, I might be able to train my brain to give rise to compassion, rather than anger, when that moment actually comes.

planets

t seems too good to be true.

There you are, your first day on the job. Your boss is a tough, work-calloused guy. He hands you a hard hat and he says . . . "Go over there and sit down."

"Then what?" you ask.

"That's it. Just go sit over there."

Your eyes widen; you wonder if he's putting you on. You glance around to check if you might be on *Candid Camera*.

"That's it?" you say. "Really? I just have to go over there and sit down on that comfortable cushion?"

The boss chews his stogie. "Yup. That's it. Do you think you can handle it?"

You scoff. This is a job that Homer Simpson could ace. The only thing that would make it better would be a steady supply of donuts.

It would be nice if meditation was really that easy.

I'd love to report that I heard about its benefits, realized how it could help me improve my divorce, and took it up immediately and wholeheartedly, like the proverbial duck to water.

Such, alas, was far from the reality.

When I went to talks, the practice seemed viable. The sessions started and ended with it, and I was in the middle of a group of supportive people who were all doing the same thing. When I was on my own, though, I found it hard to get my ass on the cushion. I would think about meditating, and nag myself about it, but more often than not I would procrastinate, or "forget," or "not get around to it." I was eager to learn about Buddhism, I wouldn't think twice about traveling an hour each way to go to talks, and I read stacks of books on the subject, but I had a hard time developing a meditation practice.

I had to ask myself why.

I couldn't claim the conventional excuses. I wasn't working nine to five; I made my own schedule and had plenty of free time. I couldn't argue that I didn't have a place to meditate, or that my living space was too cluttered. I couldn't claim that my neighborhood was too loud, or that my back couldn't support sitting still, or that people would have looked at me funny. I certainly couldn't say that I was distracted by a spouse who didn't understand, or kids who made too much noise.

In short, I had an ideal setup for a daily practice: enough quiet, enough space, enough time.

So what was the problem?

Laziness may have played a factor, and lack of motivation, but I'm not an especially lazy or unmotivated person. When

I run in the park, nobody drives a pace car in front of me, urging me on; nobody runs behind me, busting my chops if I stop. There are days when I'm sick and don't do it, or too busy with work, or just too slothful to pull on my sneakers — yet I still run pretty consistently.

What could be so hard about *sitting?*

When I stop and think about it, I can come up with a number of answers.

The most obvious one is that meditation didn't seem like *fun.* We human beings spend a lot of our time pursuing comfort and pleasure, and there was nothing obviously pleasurable about sitting. It didn't provide a rush of good sensation, like ice cream or sex. It wasn't entertaining, like a movie or a video game. In fact, it could seem like a chore, like eating some blah vegetable because it's supposed to be good for you.

What's more, the payoff was not immediately obvious. When I ran, I got that endorphin buzz, and I could feel the results: my muscles got stronger, I lost weight.

Some of the rewards of meditation *were* clear from the start. In the early days of my divorce, my mind was hugely agitated. When I meditated, I was able to get some sense that my feelings of anger and sadness and betrayal and loss were tied in with my thoughts, and — sometimes — I was able to let go of them. Occasionally I was able to transform my bitterness toward Claire into compassion for her, and that brought moments of real peace.

That should have been enough to keep me sitting, yet I still often balked.

Why?

I think meditation sometimes made me anxious because it's the opposite of the way I live most of the time.

Some people avoid silence and stillness by constantly working, by always ticking off a list of Things to Do. My problem is more Information Age: I want near-constant mental input. I'm a relentless reader. I wake up, fire up my computer, check my e-mail, catch up on various news sites. I read while I'm eating; if there's nothing else around, I'll read the back of a cereal box. And I'm in love with my iPod: I listen to it when I run, when I wait for a bus, when I'm on the subway. At night, I often watch rented DVDs, and I like to go to the movies.

For me, meditation was like going cold turkey from that constant blitz of stimulation. And that took some getting used to.

Despite my difficulties, I did finally manage to get a daily practice up and running. (Or down and sitting.)

One thing I noticed was that time expanded in an amazing way. Twenty minutes went by in a blink when I was watching TV, but those same twenty minutes often felt like an eternity when I was meditating. My friend Sherry was kind enough to give me a meditation timer, which was a big help: it chimed at the beginning and end of each session, and saved me from constantly sneaking peeks at the clock.

Getting a meditation practice going was like establishing a regular running schedule: it seemed awkward and somewhat uncomfortable for the first couple of months. It took a while for the endorphins to kick in.

The benefits were obvious when I was emotionally stirred up; I could feel myself calm down and gain some equanimity. Eventually I started to note that this equanimity seemed to be flowing into my time away from the cushion.

A couple of weeks ago, for example, I made plans to meet my friend Emily at a museum. It was the last day of a big show, and we arrived to find a huge line of patrons zigzagging through the lobby. Emily was very agitated and unhappy about that, but I just shrugged. I saw the wait as an opportunity for us to catch up with each other and talk. It's a subtle thing, but meditation can carry over into the rest of life—it helps put things in perspective. Difficulties that ordinarily loom up and threaten to stress us out, or even swamp us, just don't seem as powerful.

On the other hand, it's easy to lose mindfulness when you're busy in the world. Thich Nhat Hanh is the founder of several Buddhist retreat villages, where monks remind residents to return to awareness in a unique fashion: someone is charged with randomly ringing a bell throughout the day. When people hear it, they're supposed to stop whatever they're doing and take several deep, mindful breaths.

If we choose to find them, our regular lives can offer similar reminders. For example, I live in a tranquil neighborhood, but the house is located on a busy corner. Some comic recently observed that scientists have discovered the shortest interval of time in the universe: the moment between when a New York traffic light turns green and the cars behind the front car begin to honk. I used to get annoyed and distracted when I heard that ugly noise, but now I use it as a little reminder bell. *Return to the present. Become more aware.* You can find such opportunities everywhere:

while you're standing in a line, or filling up a glass with water, or waiting for your computer to boot up a new program.
Breathe. Relax. Be here now.

Speaking of which, you have undoubtedly heard that
meditation helps to *put you in the moment.* I have to admit that
it took me a while to begin to understand what that really
meant. *What's so great about being in the moment,* I wondered, *if
the moment might not be so great?* It's not very exciting to sit
there, and sometimes not pleasurable, especially if you've got
stuff like divorce trauma to deal with. Much of the time,
frankly, we don't want to be in the present: we want to be re-
living the past, or daydreaming about some happier future.

Again, I think about my friend Emily. She's constantly
hoping that a relationship will make her happy. When she's
single, she obsesses about finding a new love. Right now,
she's got a guy, but they're on a continual roller coaster of
mini-breakups and reunions; half the time she seems very excited about him, but half the time she's miserable. She keeps
looking forward to some time when their relationship will be
trouble-free and truly committed. She's always looking for
happiness on the horizon.

Which reminds me: at some point when I was younger, I
came up with a concept of happiness based on astronomy. I
figured that I could break life down into certain essential elements: health, financial status, love life, place to live, friendships, vocation. . . . I envisioned each of those elements as a
planet, and then pictured them rising and falling along the
horizon. Typically, some were up, but others were down; I
might—for example—be healthy and in love, but searching
for a new place to live, or looking for a new job. My idea of
true happiness was that it would occur when all the planets
reached a simultaneous peak. Now, if you know something

about astronomy, you'll recognize that such grand align-
ments *do* occur with the six inner planets of our solar system — *once every fifty or a hundred years.*

In other words, my model of happiness was just plain
nuts. Sure, everything seems to align in life on rare occa-
sions, but those conjunctions are rarely within our control. If
we wait for them to experience true happiness, we'll spend
the vast majority of our lives unhappy or dissatisfied.

Last night I was reading Charlotte Joko Beck's book
Everyday Zen, and I was startled by her chapter about hope.
We're taught that hope is a beautiful, essential human quality: it's the thing that's supposed to get us through hard times
and lift us up, like the part in a movie when the string section
swells and our protagonist takes on some grueling but ultimately heartwarming challenge, Rocky Balboa running up
the museum steps . . . When you run out of hope, all you're
left with is despair, right?

Now listen to Beck: "Actually, it's not terrible at all. A life
without hope is a peaceful, joyous, compassionate life."
Again, that shocking, counterintuitive Buddhist voice. "We
are usually living," she adds, "in vain hope for something or
someone that will make *my* life easier, more pleasant." As a
result, we "lose ninety percent of the experience of our life."

If we're always looking for happiness somewhere else,
some other time, we're never going to be *in* it.

When I'm out running, I know exactly how long the
loop is around the park, and I often find myself thinking
about how far I have to go. I think about how tired I am,
and how much energy I've got left, and the next thing I
know I'm staring down at my feet, practically counting the
steps, and the run starts to feel like *work.* A few months
back, in the heart of winter, a small older man, a total

stranger, passed me during my run. "Hey," he called out. "*Smile.*" I was startled, and could feel myself tightening up — *Who does this guy think he is?* — but then I noticed that my face was already contorted into a grim, determined mask. The stranger was right: I needed to lighten up and remind myself that I wasn't running in order to reach some finish line. The man zipped on ahead of me, leaving me grinning in his wake.

When I feel myself falling back into that abstract, determined mind of achievement, of future goals, I try to lift my head and look around. I notice the way a distant bunch of seagulls are scattered across the lake like a handful of white teeth. I see the first green shoots of crocuses spraying up out of the spring mud, not to be denied. I hear the fantastically young, cheery voices of the Beatles blending in my headphones. Sometimes I even remember to smile.

It's very easy to get caught up in believing that spiritual practice is a long run toward some distant, magical, eventual state of bliss. Zen Buddhists warn that if you become obsessed with attaining enlightenment, you likely won't find it at all. (I like the story about a student who approaches his teacher and asks how long it may take for him to reach nirvana. "Ten years," the teacher replies. "But master!" the student cries. "I have been following all of the precepts scrupulously, meditating at great length every day, and working twice as hard as the other students." The master shrugs. "Twenty years.")

Zen masters look at the spiritual journey in a very different way: they say that the path — with all its stumbles and wrong turns and screw-ups — *is* enlightenment.

This is it.

That's so easy to miss.

I'm still a rookie at meditation, and still sometimes feel as if it's a duty rather than a pleasure, but I'm starting to get interesting glimmers of what it might hold in store.

Recently, I've started meditating in the park, at the end of my run; I found a nice spot at the edge of the little lake. The other day I sat there on a sunny afternoon, gazing out at a small white boat moored in the middle of the blue water. Twenty yards away from me, a man stood operating a little radio-controlled plane, and it swooped and glided over the lake like a random thought. A group of teenagers came by and started halfheartedly tossing pebbles at some geese. A woman passed by pushing a little sleeping child in a stroller. An old woman crouched at the water's edge, taking a photo of a startlingly white egret perched on a dead branch rising up out of the water.

I noticed that I felt some annoyance arise inside of me when I saw the man sending his little airplane across my serene view. I noticed that some fear arose in me when I saw the teenagers, and then some anger. I noticed that some compassion arose in me when I saw the mother and her child, and the old woman. I decided to try to let go of my judgments, and I just sat calmly, under a shady tree, taking it all in. I wasn't mourning my divorce, or worrying about some date, or even planning what to have for dinner. I watched the breeze lightly brush the surface of the water, and I breathed and sat with what was in front of me. I noticed how the man with the plane was delighting his two small children, and my heart warmed toward him. I noticed that the teenagers were not really malicious, just awkward and alienated from the rest of the scene, and I felt some compassion for them. I sat and looked out across the water. After a few minutes I felt my heart swell with a spacious, serene contentment. And I sensed that this powerful, expansive feeling might be always available, whenever I cared to tap into it.

When I finally got up to leave, I thought of another man sitting beneath a tree some twenty-five hundred years ago, boldly discovering a whole new relationship between himself and his world, and I was grateful.

◻

Yesterday I had a breakthrough. For a long time I'd been imagining encountering my ex-wife again, and trying to prepare myself to avoid doing anything I might regret. This time, though, deep in a meditative state, I was able to picture myself taking a walk with her. I could ask her how she's doing, and avoid bringing up any past resentments and complaints. I could reconnect to the times we felt so close to each other, and to envision that we might even still be friends.

To play devil's advocate, it's possible that I might have reached that point without any Buddhist teachings or meditation. After all, as the saying goes, *time heals all wounds.* It's been two years, and maybe it's just time for the petty grudges to lose their grip, leaving better memories behind.

Here's the catch, though: maybe time would let past troubles fade, but it won't inoculate me against making the same mistakes the next time.

That's one reason why I'm training now.

where there's a will

Running and meditating still require effort. I still have to pull on the sneakers and leave the house, and I still have to get myself onto that cushion. These activities require *intention*, and I'd like to tell you three little stories about that.

◌

First, a big group of people comes together in a church basement and they sit for an hour chanting and praying for world peace.

(Not a very plot-filled or exciting story, I admit—but we'll come back to it.)

◌

Second, a toddler wanders out into a busy city street. A passing man, moved by the plight of the little stranger, recognizes the value of this other life, selflessly dashes out into the traffic, scoops the child up, and carries him to safety.

In an alternate version of this story, the same child wanders out into the street, but this time a different man passes by. He sees the danger the child is in, imagines what glory and reward he might get if he saves the kid—a front page photo in the tabloids? Money from the grateful parents?—and dashes out and performs the rescue.

◩

Lastly, a true story. Back when I was in college, I took a course with a rather eccentric professor about The Philosophy of Music. It ended up being about The Meaning of Life, which was fine with most of his students, a bunch of young people enthralled by big ideas. Here was one of his homework assignments: Try to do something you think is impossible.

I can't remember how I came up with my experiment, but it seems to have anticipated my interest in Buddhism by some twenty-five years. I told myself, *I'm going to try to be compassionate with every single person I meet for one whole day.* Such a modest challenge may hardly seem impossible, but I failed pretty quickly, and not for the reasons I anticipated. Things went fine for the first hour or two: I smiled at my roommates, cleaned some dirty dishes that someone else had left in the kitchen, said a cheerful Hello to the girl behind the counter where I bought my morning bagel. . . . And then several hours later I was in the middle of some other class and realized that I had completely forgotten about my special assignment.

◩

Let's return to the first two scenarios.

Religious people of many stripes believe in the power of prayer—believe, that is, that it's a meritorious activity in and of itself, and even that it has a real power to change the world.

Personally, I've always taken a hard-edged, skeptical approach to that idea. I don't believe that praying for world peace has any effect whatsoever on people on the other side of the planet. (People with bitterly entrenched tribal grievances are not going to suddenly lay down their weapons and live together in harmony just because some guy in Brooklyn has taken the trouble to chant a few words.) My gut reaction has always been: *If you have the time and drive and resources to pray together with other people, why not use all that energy to effect some real political change?*

Likewise, in the scenario with the child in traffic, a traditional Buddhist would say that the spiritual intention of the rescuer makes a fundamental difference. My gut reaction: *Who cares what the intention is, so long as the child gets saved?*

After practicing Buddhism for a while, though, I look at all three stories differently.

I look at my experiment in compassion and see that it failed, not because being compassionate is so difficult in and of itself, but simply because my intention to stay mindful was not strong enough.

I look at the group of people praying, and I'm not busy being skeptical about whether those prayers have some magical wish-fulfilling power. Instead, I see a group of people who are boosting their intention to do real good. (My Buddhist friend Tim experienced a similar change of view: "I was motivated to adjust my somewhat skeptical attitude towards prayer when I was told that the Tibetan word for prayer translates as 'wish path.' I just love that. Essentially, in this context, a prayer is a message to your own mind . . . an intention . . . a direction to remind yourself you want to take.")

I look at the two different rescuers of the child, and I'm not concerned about their motivation in that particular moment. I figure that the man who is acting out of compassion—and following his wish path—will likely extend that intention and perform other, less-spectacular acts of kindness throughout his day, whereas the other guy—well, how many opportunities will he have to act the hero?

The point, in short, is that developing a positive intention is important because it gets you ready to act in a kind way when the opportunity arises—and if you're ready, it arises all the time.

I'm beginning to understand that my drawing of a hard-edged line between imaginary thought and "real" action might be a mistake. As Geshe Kelsang Gyatso points out, all human creations had their origin in our imaginations. Cathedrals and computers didn't just magically appear; someone had to think of them, and draw up plans. And then, of course, they had to follow through on an intention to build them.

One of the major values of meditation is that it allows us to cultivate and strengthen our intention. And then we can do some good—or at least try not to screw things up.

anatomy of an e-mail

A year into my Buddhist journey, I came home to my new apartment and found a stack of mail in the front hall. Cell phone bill, Chinese takeout menu, bank statement . . . my heart froze. I picked up a small cream-colored envelope, the size of a wedding invitation. I knew who it was from immediately, before I even read a word. I stared at my soon-to-be-ex-wife's name, and then I stared at her new address. And then I gingerly carried the envelope inside, as if it might be radioactive.

For the previous eight months I had had no contact with Claire. No phone calls, no e-mails, nothing. The previous New Year's Eve, motivated by a book on love by Thich Nhat Hanh, I had written her a heartfelt apology for my failings that had contributed to the failure of our marriage, and I wished her great happiness, even if it would be with someone else. She never replied.

Now my heart was thumping. I sat in the dark for a moment, clutching the unopened envelope, trying to steel myself for what I might be about to read. My monkey mind ran wild. After all this time of deadly silence, was she finally going to tender an apology of her own—or at least accept mine?

Maybe the letter was about something else. Despite my best efforts to be realistic, despite all the work I had put into acceptance of impermanence and change, I couldn't avoid one big question: Was it possible that she had changed her mind? I grasped wildly for the next branch. If she wanted to get back together, could I possibly forgive her treatment of me during the past year?

I was reeling. I took a couple of deep breaths, tried to calm myself, and then turned on a light and tore open the envelope.

The note inside was only three sentences long. It said that she hoped I was well, and that there were a couple of things she wanted to discuss with me, and she wondered how it would be most comfortable to do so (by letter, e-mail, phone, or in person).

I stared at the card, utterly baffled. I read those few words over and over, trying my hardest to tease out any hidden meanings, but the thing was more cryptic than the da Vinci code. I even stared at the stamp. It showed two bluebirds sitting on one branch. Their bodies were turned away from each other, but their heads leaned together. *What could it possibly mean?*

I spent twenty-four hours wrestling with my imagination. I didn't think it could be a legal development—we had already hashed out a separation agreement and now it was just a matter of running out the clock. But she had used the word "discuss." Maybe, after all this time, she was finally willing to sit down with me and talk. Maybe we could try to make some sense of what had happened between us.

On the other hand, maybe she wanted to deliver more bad news. I thought of movie scenes in which a character calls a hopeful ex-spouse, only to drop a bomb: *I want to tell you something before you hear it from someone else: I'm getting remarried.*

And yet . . . she had mentioned the possibility of getting together "in person." What if—despite her seeming coldness—she actually missed me? What if she regretted her rash departure and wanted to give us another chance?

Despite my best Buddhist efforts to stay calm, the suspense was killing me. I sat down and wrote an e-mail.

> Dear Claire, after eight months of complete silence between us, I was very surprised to get home yesterday and find your mysterious card. It reminded me of the famous Jewish telegram: "Start worrying. Details to follow." Now, of course, I'm trying to imagine what you could possibly want to discuss— and why you didn't just say what it was . . . Could you at least give me a clue?

◖

I had to wait another twenty-three hours to find out.

Claire finally sent a brief e-mail to say that she had gotten in touch because she was going out of the country for a while and wanted to let me know that she planned to put her divorce paperwork in order before she left.

That was it. I was disappointed and bewildered. I wrote back.

Why on Earth would you send me a cryptic note like
that, and ask whether I might feel "comfortable"
"discuss"ing this mysterious subject in person, and
churn me up totally unnecessarily, when you could
simply have sent me an e-mail giving me this information—which, come to think of it—I don't need in
the first place?

◁

I had spent the past year working very hard on a new
approach to life, and hoped that Claire might have developed
some new insight too, but we fell right back into the old
pattern. She wrote back with a blistering e-mail, which
complained that I took everything the worst way and followed up with various unpleasant epithets.

Our communication spiraled out of control from there,
into those familiar flares of anger, that seemingly inevitable
nuclear meltdown.

That night I went to a Buddhist talk. I needed it, like a
recovering alcoholic who desperately seeks the support of a
meeting. The topic, ironically, was Inner Cool. It was basi-
cally a repeat of the first talk I had ever gone to, Matthew's
discussion of How to Deal with Anger. I sat there, mortified.
Hadn't I learned *anything?*

When I got home, I wrote to Claire again.

How about if we try to do something a little different? How about if instead of saying mean things to
each other, I look at your card again, and work on
seeing a better interpretation of how you handled
things? If I see you trying to be considerate of my

feelings, and asking how I'd feel most comfortable communicating with you? How about if I say, I'm sorry? And how about if you try to see that maybe the way you dealt with this might have gotten my hopes up that we could finally talk? How about if you try to understand that I was disappointed, and very emotionally shaken up to finally hear from you, instead of angry? How about if you say, I'm sorry? Wouldn't that be better than all this anger?

◻

Claire's response contained only fury.

◻

Another disastrous interchange.

If you're going through a divorce right now, I suspect you may be shaking your head in sad recognition. Quite possibly, your situation is more dire, with more frequent conflicts. Somehow, you have to keep it together in order be able to negotiate with your spouse. You go into conversations with the best intentions, determined to remain civil, yet somehow things still get out of hand.

A week before our time together ended, Claire and I tried going to another therapist. The woman listened to us talk about our problems. She looked at both of us, then said, "I have a feeling that it may be too late to save this marriage."

I was shocked. This was a licensed professional therapist, whose job was supposedly to help people improve their lives and relationships, but she seemed ready to throw in the towel after just one session! In retrospect, I'm still shocked, but at least I can see what gave her such grave doubts.

I've mentioned Shunryu Suzuki's emphasis on staying open and fresh to every situation, what he called "beginner's mind." I think the therapist saw two people who had completely lost that flexibility. Claire and I were too agitated, convinced of each other's faults, unwilling to concede our own, unable to see the good qualities in each other, unable to give, to compromise, to bend. We were saturated with what I might call "petrified mind." We were so sure that the other was to blame that we had turned our marriage to stone. To return to Matthew's subway analogy, we could only see the spouse sitting next to us in one way: as a *problem*.

We sat in that therapist's office like an Israeli and a Palestinian, and the poor woman saw little hope for détente. I'm not saying that as some kind of glib metaphor. As I write this, various wars rage around the world, and in every one, both sides are convinced that they're completely in the right. The result? Thousands of dead children, thousands of destroyed homes. Absolute belief can easily become a curse. The history of the twentieth century shows that nothing is more dangerous. From Hitler to Mao, from Stalin to Pol Pot, unbelievable carnage has been wreaked on the planet by people who were absolutely, rigidly convinced of their own righteousness. Imagine what a different world this could be if our leaders could be more open to other views, more compassionate, more willing to see the world afresh. What if all of the fanatical, furious believers were able to pause now and then and tell themselves, *Not necessarily so*?

This is a book about divorce and not a polemic about world politics, but there's no separation between the small truths and the big ones. The road to world peace starts with being able to look at other riders on the subway and to see them in a new way.

When I look back on my last e-mail interchange with Claire, I have to admit that I did a lousy job of seeing my spouse afresh. We both did.

I approached her initial note, which was in itself polite and bland, with a huge amount of suspicion. She, in turn, was eager to pounce on the faintest whiff of anger. We both went into the exchange expecting the worst. (When things are at this stage, e-mail is probably a bad idea. It's often hard to interpret tone; a wry joke may get taken as a serious affront. There's no eye contact or body language that might reveal the true intent. And worse, it's so easy to reply in haste, to fire off an angry response.)

In retrospect, I can see several ways in which I could have handled things better. I might have had the guts to try to summon up all of my new patience, and agree to see Claire in person. That would have been nerve-wracking and emotionally risky, but maybe some of the love we still felt for each other might have had a chance to shine through. At the least, I could have waited longer before I responded, could have meditated to calm my mind and to build compassion for her, could have made greater efforts to strip my e-mails of any possible indications of anger. I could have sat and tried to see things from her perspective. After the Buddhist talk, I understood that I could have approached the exchange in an entirely different way.

Who knows what might have happened? Maybe we could have let ourselves see the good in each other again, the bright loving core that had brought us together in the first place. In any case, it was too late. We had screwed up. Again.

I cursed myself. *Idiot! You put a year of work into learning how to act better, and then let it all down in one stupid exchange.*

I had to force myself to remember what my new teachers had told me. Buddhism is not about figuring everything out, or about being perfect. It's a continual path. There will most certainly be setbacks, and lapses, and mistakes. Great skillfulness is required, and developing it takes time. It's a *practice*. And it requires courage, persistence, and great patience.

(A sense of humor also helps. I love the genre of *New Yorker* cartoons devoted to exhausted seekers who have just struggled to the top of a mountain, where they ask a guru to reveal life's answers. In a classic by Peter Steiner, the frustrated guru responds, "If I knew the secret of life, would I be sitting in a cave in my underpants?")

Yes, I had screwed up my end of the exchange with Claire, but it could have been worse. I could have released all my pent-up frustration from the past year, could have said all the hurtful things I had been itching to say. I didn't, though — I was able to exercise some degree of restraint. And I tried to open up a wider view.

I'm reminded of a legendary Buddhist practitioner named Geshe Ben Gungyal, who gauged his progress in a unique way. During the course of the day, when a negative thought arose he would place a black pebble in front of him. When a positive thought arose, he would place a white pebble. At the end of each day, he counted the pebbles. If there were more black ones, he would resolve to try harder. If there were more white ones, he would allow himself a little praise. It took him years to get to a point where he could pass one whole day without any black pebbles.

In *Zen Mind, Beginner's Mind*, Shunryu Suzuki refers to a Buddhist scripture saying that there are four different kinds of horses, ranging from a horse that will obey its master before it even sees a shadow of the whip, to a second type that will respond before the whip reaches its skin, to a third that will run when it feels some pain, to a fourth horse that will perform only when the pain penetrates all the way down to the marrow of its bones. "When we hear this story," says Suzuki, "almost all of us want to be the best horse. . . . If you think the aim of Zen practice is to train you to become one of the best horses, you will have a big problem. . . . If you practice Zen in the right way, it does not matter whether you are the best horse or the worst one. When you consider the mercy of Buddha, how do you think Buddha will feel about the four kinds of horses? He will have more sympathy for the worst one."

For the past year, I thought I had done a pretty good job of stabilizing my life again, of finding some measure of peace. Now another storm had blown up, and for a week after, I was badly shaken. Anger, hope, disappointment, resentment, confusion, sadness, they all came rushing back. I remember watching TV late one night. In the middle of a show I turned off the set and lay there on my couch, in the dark, soaking in the silence, watching the shadows of the trees play across my apartment windows. I felt bruised and exhausted. I was grieving all over again.

I had new motivation to plant my seat on the cushion. And I did.

I soon realized three things I had not known till then.

First, under all of my anger and disillusionment, I discovered that I still loved Claire. And I realized that—as thoughts can't hurt the clear sky of the mind—so all my frustration and resentment, our arguments and misunderstandings, the passage of time, the work of lawyers, even Claire's cold silences and willful unkindnesses, *nothing* had spoiled the love I felt, true gold which could not be defiled. I still had that capacity in my heart, and divorce could never take it away.

When we experience a bad breakup, we tend to think that we're suffering to the same degree to which we loved, or even to believe, as Simon and Garfunkel ironically put it, that "If I never loved, I never would have cried." Buddhism, as usual, says something surprising and counterintuitive: that real love is *never* the cause of suffering.

I realized that I had built up such a negative picture of Claire for one futile, self-deceptive purpose: to try to devalue the immensity of our loss.

And, last but not least, I finally recognized that it was time to let our marriage go.

other voices

I wondered what life is like for Buddhist practitioners with different divorce stories, particularly ones that involved kids or frequent contact with ex-spouses, so I set out to interview a number of other people. I didn't prescreen their stories to judge whether I found them interesting enough or in line with my own ideas. In every single case, I found their stories moving and inspirational.

Take Jessica, whose marriage ended in dramatic fashion. Just before September 11, 2001, she found out that her husband had been cheating. The day after that more publicly devastating event, she kicked him out of the house. "My whole world had caved in," she recalls. And she had two kids, including a seriously disabled young son she had to carry up nine flights of stairs because the elevator was out.

When asked how Buddhism affected her relationship with her ex-husband, Jessica's response is startling in its directness, even if she's (mostly) joking. "If I hadn't started studying it, he would probably be dead. I hated him so much."

Luckily, though, Jessica didn't act on her rage; she discovered an alternative. "I had been a Buddhist admirer for a long time. I went to India and Nepal in 1985 — at that point it seemed inaccessible to me, but I saw that Buddhists seemed calm and happy." Much later, she was moved by a book on anger by Thich Nhat Hanh. And then, a couple of months after the end of her marriage, Jessica discovered that there was a Buddhist center just three doors down from her apartment building. "The second I walked in," she says, "I felt, 'This is home.'" She adds that the teachings felt familiar "because I had already learned a lot as the mother of a special needs child — like Exchanging Self with Others."

She started attending talks, but in the meantime, she had to see her ex on a regular basis. "I thought, *This is the last person I want to deal with, and I can't get rid of him.*" She felt a powerful urge to blame her husband for their troubles, but found a new perspective starting to emerge. "He was such a prick, and I didn't want to let him off the hook, but I realized that he could not *inherently* be a prick. That took some of the heat off him and allowed me to see him with some compassion, and see him as a suffering being. And the Buddhism helped me focus on the anger as a delusion in my own mind. My delusions were running rampant, but I'd had no idea. With self-cherishing, everything's about *you.* Your partner doesn't fulfill all your wishes and that's disappointing. Now I know that another person can't give that to me."

Jessica has studied Buddhism for four and a half years, and has found that she is able to use it to transform her relationship with her ex-husband. "I have tools to deal with all sorts of situations that I didn't have before. He can still get under my skin, and I'll get angry for a second, but I can let it go. It's like martial arts: I apply dharma in the moment."

Like me, Jessica wonders how things might have been different if she had discovered Buddhism before her divorce. "I've thought many times, *What would have happened to our marriage?* I wonder how much my changing could effect another person's change."

Jessica discovered Buddhism too late to find out if it could have helped her save her marriage, but it has had a major positive effect on her divorce. "The anger in my system was physically poisoning me," she concludes. "I feel like dharma saved my life."

♩

Mike's wife ended their twenty-five-year marriage three years ago. "I was incredibly hurt," he recalls. He started studying Buddhism just a year ago, but reports that, "It has helped me beyond my wildest imagination, from dealing with my ex to dealing with our two kids."

His divorce came through less than a year ago. Like Jessica, Mike had new tools for dealing with that traumatic experience. "I remember times when a strong e-mail came from my ex and I literally shook with wanting to send an equally strong e-mail back to her—but I didn't retaliate. I never responded, and whatever that issue was became not an issue." This was a major insight. "By not fighting back, I saw that we could have a very different relationship. I see a real softening in my ex—she knows that it's important to me not to be aggressive, not to lie.

"I use my ex as a real motivation for my practice," Mike adds. "Once, for example, I thought I had helped my daughter with her homework. My ex is a teacher and she called up to complain. I could really feel it in the top of my chest, that Me? *Me?* Then I used that feeling in meditation to analyze that strong sense of myself—and it drifted into nothingness. That made me feel so much better. I took an adverse condition and meditated to see if it could help me—and it did."

Ironically, Mike now feels that his relationship with his ex-wife is better than ever. "My love for my ex is at its most powerful, deepest, more satisfying than it was when we were married. It's not a love of wanting her back—it's a love for somebody who was very meaningful to my life and will continue to be."

That love recently survived two big challenges.

First, his wife announced that she is getting remarried. Thanks to his new perspective, Mike has found that he can even extend his good feelings to her new partner. "I can love her fiancé too, because he's making her happy." Two days before our interview, Mike had to deal with both of them in a potentially difficult situation. The two announced that they were moving to an adjoining state. Mike decided to look for a new apartment somewhere nearby, so he could be close to his children. He drove out to meet with the new couple. "I could see my ex-wife coming down the stairs with her hair wet from a shower, and I could think, *Oh, this is where you live now.* That was all of it. And then, for three hours I drove around with [her new fiancé] looking for a place for me to move to. I had nothing but kindness in my heart for him for taking the time to do that. I felt no jealousy. I think of jealousy as being just a *nothing* emotion; it's not useful for anything."

If Mike's transformation may sound a bit too good to be true after just a year of Buddhist practice, I should point out that he has new reason for optimism and joy. "I went through the exact reverse of a midlife crisis," he says. "I was in my mid-forties when I separated, and I could have gone for young women and one-night stands." Instead, he found a new relationship with a woman he met through an online dating service. She is also a practicing Buddhist, also divorced. Mike says that they are experiencing a much deeper, more intimate relationship.

It's clear that one thing that has contributed to this improvement is Mike's new perspective on his own responsibility for his failed marriage. "I was the master of passive-aggressiveness. And one of the downfalls of my marriage was my desirous attachment for other women. My relationships in the past were selfish and attached and based on making Mike happy."

In his new relationship, he says, "There's a huge contrast with where I was. The way I resolve conflicts is totally different—I can't imagine raising my voice. (With my ex, I would swear at her first, then ignore her for two weeks.) If you're thinking of the other person, it's really hard to argue about something. There's a goal of unconditional love."

Like Jessica, Mike has even managed to find a positive side to his regular part-time separation from his kids: it gives him time to pursue his new spiritual path.

〇

Joyce's story is quite different: she initiated her divorce based on her own dissatisfaction. She had discovered Buddhism well before that time, and she had undergone a lot of turmoil before she even met her husband.

Joyce is a professional musician, and her career fed into a destructive need for perfection. "College felt like a bumper car experience," she remembers. "Everything was about per-forming, about playing everything perfectly, about fitting in. I was always trying to please my teachers. I was always try-ing to fit into others' ideas, to be the perfect student, perfect player, perfect daughter. Inside, I was getting very stressed out. I was having panic attacks, but didn't know what they were. I was at a topnotch conservatory, but I felt lost and inadequate. I was really unhappy. I went on to play in an orchestra, and I felt really isolated. I got sick and thought I might die."

As I mentioned earlier, Joyce's Buddhist studies have given her an interesting perspective on this rough period of her life. "There was tons of self-cherishing and self-grasping," she says now. "I was obsessed with my own identity. Even low self-esteem is self-cherishing."

Joyce's marriage seemed to fit into her pattern of trying to meet expectations. "I had just gotten out of a very tumul-tuous relationship," she recalls. "I was devastated, but fell into a new one very quickly. The new guy was smitten with me, and very forceful, and I ended up living with him and then getting married. I really cared about him, and thought he was fantastic. And I thought I could be 'the right person.' The first year was kind of rosy, but within two years I think I knew; we had gotten together without knowing each other really well, and now we were finding uglier parts of each other. I stayed married as long as I did because I loved his family so much and because I felt like I belonged some-where, but by year three it felt kind of dead. I didn't feel like he was recognizing me anymore—we had come together for wrong reasons and now we were growing out of it."

Despite these troubles, the marriage went on for three more years before Joyce finally decided to end it. "When I moved out," she says, "it was so painful because I really cared about him and didn't want to hurt him, but we had come to a point where we only made each other unhappy and that was our only way of interacting. Honestly, I think if I hadn't had Buddhist teachings on the nature of mind, I think I would have continued to think I had to conform to what other people expected of me."

Joyce explains that she had long been casually interested in Buddhism. "It seemed to make sense. I had a high school teacher who led a meditation class, and we read *Siddhartha* [Herman Hesse's novel about the Buddha's life story]." During Joyce's marriage, her exposure to Buddhism grew wider. "I heard Thich Nhat Hanh speak live. I had no idea who he was, but I was really moved. I was struck by how peaceful, still, and quiet he was—and how foreign that seemed to me." Another influence was reading Tina Turner's autobiography. (Turner is a practicing Buddhist.) "That really affected me," Joyce recalls. "I saw that I wasn't the person I had set out to be—and there wasn't anybody to blame. I decided in earnest to meditate and learn about Buddhism." Soon she discovered a local Buddhist center and stepped up her practice.

That practice would ultimately stand her in good stead. "When I moved out, I felt totally lost and scared and helpless. My husband said, 'You're not going to survive on your own.' Later, I experienced a lot of guilt—I felt that I had inadvertently manipulated him. If the dharma hadn't taught me that my karma was the result of my own actions, and that I was responsible for my own happiness and suffering, I don't know how I would have survived.

"The most significant thing Buddhist teachings have taught me is that another person is not responsible for my state of mind, so I'm not externalizing another person as my source of happiness. I don't always feel I have to be right, and I'm more accepting of others, and of situations, and of myself. I would never have done this before, but now I look to see what I'm contributing to the situation if things get difficult with another person. That's definitely a productive way to improve my relationships with other people across the board."

ᓚ

Cordelia knew that her nine-year relationship was in trouble when she and her boyfriend were out with a group of people and he introduced her to an attractive redhead as "my friend." Not long after, he left. "I was so devastated and hurt and angry," she recalls. "We were the couple everybody thought would stay together." After the breakup, Cordelia reports, "I was miserable. I thought my life would end."

Prior to that time, she had studied Buddhism as well as other spiritual traditions including Sufism, Quakerism, and Christic mysticism, and she had some experience with meditation. "My practice stopped me from doing things I would later regret," she says. "And it gave me the ability to step back a little from my feelings. When you have really big feelings, it's like they're bigger than you—you're lost in them. With spiritual practice, though, there's a decrease in misery. You can see that your consciousness is bigger than them." Without her practice, she says, "I think I would have been more crazy with grief, doing a lot more blaming, fighting, and yelling. But I had an ability to sit still in the middle of something tumultuous."

She found herself sustained by a volume by Buddhist meditation teacher Jack Kornfield called *Buddha's Little*

Instruction Book. Cordelia kept opening the book to one particular sentence that read: "Life is so difficult, how can we be anything but kind?" "That had a lot of meaning for me," she says. "It helped me put my feelings in the context of human suffering. It was talking not just about my life, or [my boyfriend's] life, but *life*. This combats the idea we have in the West that life should be nice all the time—that puts a lot of pressure on us."

As she speaks about accepting suffering, Cordelia points to a famous Buddhist parable. A woman whose child had suddenly died was so overwhelmed with grief that she went around carrying the dead boy in her arms, asking the other villagers for medicine. With sadness, they told her that they had no medicine that could help her, but they suggested that she go see a physician named the Buddha. "Master," she implored him, "please give me a medicine that will cure my child." He told her that she should go out and gather a mustard seed. "The seed must be taken from a house where no one has lost a child, husband, parent, or friend." She went from house to house in her village, but couldn't find a single one where no one had died. She went to other towns, without success. Finally, realizing that death falls on all houses, she accepted this truth and was able to bury her child.

Along with suffering and impermanence, Cordelia's experience showed her a lot about how desirous attachment works, and changed her attitude about relationships. "I'm not so willing to get swept away at the beginning," she says. "Spiritual practice has taught me a lot about how we convince ourselves of things because we want them to be true. At first, the sex is great and that's a real high. That doesn't really mean anything about the relationship in the future, but your psyche tries to hang on to that. I understand how you can lose yourself and make bad decisions because love makes you feel so good."

How does she think her practice will affect her next relationship? "I'd rather have something kinder, less hungry, less desperate. I want to be really honest and present. Sitting and watching is so useful in terms of seeing how we deceive ourselves and other people. If I can see that in myself, that's going to lead to a better relationship. We're in a culture where you're sort of *supposed* to be selfish, but when you see how much being selfish ultimately hurts you, it's easier to resist. Kindness is so important. It's not logical—you can decide to be kind even if the other person is being an asshole. I think if two people really decide to be kind to each other, they can find their way through everything."

◪

Beth's story provides a particularly inspirational example of the redemptive power of patience and compassion.

In 2005, her six-year marriage underwent a change when she and her husband entered different graduate schools and their relationship became temporarily long-distance. On July 4, that separation took a drastic turn: he came to her and announced that he had found someone else and wanted a divorce.

"I was bowled over," Beth says. "But I dug in my heels and said, 'No, we have to work on this.'" Her husband had "ventured" earlier in their marriage—a one-night stand—but they had stayed together and worked through it, and she hoped they would be able to weather this new infidelity.

Even before his sudden announcement, her husband's behavior had grown increasingly troubled. He had undergone bouts of manic behavior, checked himself into a hospital for suicidal thoughts, and began drinking heavily to calm his agitated states. "We were in a blender of business," as Beth puts it. Ultimately, part of the reason for her husband's instability became clear to both of them: he was diagnosed with a hyperthyroid condition, which sometimes includes manic/depressive psychological symptoms.

This medical explanation gave Beth reason for hope. She asked her husband to end his affair, or at least to put it on hold so that they could resolve their own situation first. He refused. And he insisted that he still wanted the divorce.

If you want a good example of impermanence, this is it: Beth found that the man she had married had become "a completely different person with a completely different personality." She realized that she could only deal with the situation from her own side.

She had begun experiencing anxiety attacks after her husband's shocking announcement, and she started seeing a therapist who prescribed pills. But she had also had some prior exposure to Buddhist thought, and she turned to it in earnest after her marriage fell apart. Eventually, she decided that it would be better to calm her agitated mind with meditation, rather than medication. And she began studying Buddhism in earnest.

"I had picked up Pema Chödrön's book *Start Where You Are* four years ago. I read it again last year, and that led to reading other books and reading a ton on the Internet. It was like a smorgasbord—All You Can Eat."

Beth's process of coming to terms with the divorce was a gradual one. "It took me a while to resolve the anger," she says. "I didn't want to get angry with my husband at first because I was worried about his health. As I studied, it became easier to let go of that *How could he do this to me?*" She regained her life through a new regimen of Buddhist practice, running, and yoga. What I find especially inspiring about Beth's story is that she quickly expanded her focus beyond her own suffering. "I would find myself in yoga poses completely crying for my husband—I realized that he and his parents were suffering so much and I wished I could take that away."

Beth's own parents divorced when she was young. "I saw my mom carry a lot of bitterness for a long time." When her own divorce came, she was determined to remain friends with her husband. "We had shared some of the most amazing times of our lives together."

Beth's divorce was finalized last year. Her new Buddhist studies have helped put that failure in a different perspective. "I've been able to look back and know that the affair was an effect and not the root cause of the downfall of our marriage. It was a fifty-fifty thing, and I had to take my responsibility." After she read Geshe Kelsang Gyatso's book *Transform Your Life,* she thought *"Oh my God, I never gave freely.* This was a huge realization. I didn't communicate. I wasn't always honest with my feelings. I often didn't speak, and thought, *If I act, he'll pick up on what I'm thinking;* I would expect him to know. You can't expect people to pick up on those things. And I gave, but expected something back. I didn't realize that then."

With the divorce, the fact of impermanence really hit home. Beth's early family experience had been difficult, and she had become very attached to her husband and to his family. "They were a traditional, together family, something I had grasped for all my life. When he told me about the divorce, one of my first thoughts was, *Oh my God, I'm going to lose his family.* The harder I grasped [to the marriage], afraid

I would lose something, we just slowly fell apart. Now I'm starting to let go of this idea that I need to hold on. Now I say, *Whatever our relationship is, it's okay. Things come together and fall apart.*"

Beth remains close with her husband's family, and she recognized how they were also devastated by the divorce. She sees her intention to be friends with her ex post-divorce as, "not just for me. This is giving freely. My intention is to do this for him and his folks and his sisters. I hope his family will be able to mend."

And she recognizes that her ex-husband will have to make his own way. "I see him suffer from self-grasping and self-cherishing and from the drinking," she says. "But you can't tell a person—they have to come to these realizations for themselves."

Even so, she decided that there was still something she could do for him. "About three weeks ago, I thought, *I need to let him know that I totally forgive him.*" With her hands, she makes a gesture of opening her heart. The day before I interviewed her, she had gotten together with her ex-husband for the first time in a long while. "We had a wonderful lunch together. I told him, 'I forgive you, and I'm sorry—when I gave I totally expected something in return.' He broke down in tears and said that he never wanted to hurt me, that he always wanted my happiness.

"I've made changes and look at things so differently now," she concludes. "And I think he sees me as more relaxed, more comfortable, as *released* from whatever we had that went bad."

still my best friend

I've explained a number of insights that helped me with my divorce, and I hope that you can use them to forge a more positive path of your own. I wish you the best of luck, or—to put it in a more Buddhist way—I wish that you will become free of suffering and find true happiness.

Before I go, I'd like to take a moment to look back and reflect on the path behind me.

Remember how I opened this book by mentioning people with serious illnesses who talked about their suffering as a gift? I do (sometimes) manage to see my divorce that way. It's not a gift I would have chosen, and definitely not one I would be pleased to receive again. There's no way around it: divorce *sucks*.

But there's a certain lightness, a freedom that came with discovering that I could go through a tough life experience and come out on the other side. That gives me a measure of confidence that I'll be able to face other big challenges. And, like Dr. Siegel's cancer patients, I don't sweat the small stuff as much. I haven't miraculously stopped wasting any of my allotted time—I still watch the occasional sitcom, and I haven't done all I can to improve my relationships with loved ones—but I'm working on building a richer life, one small step at a time. I try not to place my center of happiness in external things I can't control: not in money, or possessions, or success, or fame. I'm not holding out for a fairytale romance. I try to take responsibility for my own happiness, and work toward creating it within.

I'm thankful that I received my wake-up call at a point when I can still alter the course of my life. I hope that I'll be able to improve my future relationships. And I hope that by the time I'm about to die, I'll be able to look back on the journey with fewer regrets, and to accept my death with greater equanimity and peace.

Since I know only one side of the story, I have had to struggle to understand what happened to my marriage, and I'm facing the possibility that I may never fully understand. In the meantime, all I can do is try to accept, and to forgive. Over time, with the help of Buddhist practice, the anger and resentment is fading, leaving mainly sadness and regret at the sheer cock-up my wife and I made of things. I wonder why we couldn't have been a little less stubborn and proud, a little more kind and giving. A little more willing to stick things out. Of course, the sadness and regret are not helpful either, unless I use them as motivation for better future behavior.

I hope—sincerely—that my ex-wife has found the happiness she was searching for. And that we'll both manage to do a better job of loving, the next time around.

For now, I'd like to leave you with one last insight, a powerful message about divorce.

Clearly, pursuing a Buddhist path involves recognizing that we don't get to wisdom and freedom without going through some rough patches. We have to learn to see that suffering is a major part of life, understand that it comes from within, resolve to free ourselves from it, and take action to train our minds.

And so Buddhism offers one more surprising, counterintuitive notion: *We should be very grateful for the people in our lives who seem the most difficult. They're blessings in disguise. Without them, how would we ever make spiritual progress?*

In this sense, I suppose I could say that my ex-wife is *still* my best friend.

♩

When I was a kid, I studied Greek mythology. I'm not sure why, but one story made a very deep impression on me. Orpheus, a wandering musician, falls in love with a beautiful maiden named Eurydice. They marry and are able to love each other for a time, but then she's carried off by Hades, the king of the Underworld. Orpheus is so grief-stricken, so in love, that he dares what no man has ever dared: he travels down to the Underworld to bring her back. Hades is so impressed by Orpheus's courage and his singing that he consents to let Eurydice travel back with him to the upper realm. There's one condition, though: on the journey up, Orpheus must never look at her. They make their way up toward the light, but at the last moment, he turns to her and she slips away forever.

Despite my Buddhist training, my slowly increasing mindfulness and peace, I still empathize with Orpheus's suffering. Every few months I still have those dreams in which I go back and find Claire, and we're reunited, and once again I experience a deep, selfless side of our love. Then I wake up and she is gone.

The next time I see her in that sad, dark place, I hope I'll be able to deliver one big small message:

Thank you.

a plan of action

This book has introduced many Buddhist different concepts and insights. Here's a summary of specific, practical steps you can take to improve the general temper of a divorce — and, hopefully, the tenor of your future relationships:

Resolve to do no harm.

The bottom line. Buddhist practice requires this fundamental oath, and it's essential to try to follow it in divorce. A breakup feeds feelings of rejection and hurt, and a compensating desire to project the pain outward. Before undertaking any speech or action that might hurt your partner, take the time to check your motivation. Make a conscious resolution to avoid criticism, sarcasm, insult, and injury.

Refrain from acting from anger.

Acting from anger always has negative consequences. If you practice meditation, you can see that angry thoughts are just thoughts—they don't have to determine your behavior. You don't have to deny that you're angry, or try to repress your anger. Allow yourself to sit with it; explore how it comes from a feeling of injury to your self; then let it go. Learn to put a breathing space between the flare of feeling and the angry action; use that helpful pause to discover alternative ways to act.

Practice patience.

The antidote to anger. If you see external things or people as intrinsic problems, life offers endless opportunities to get annoyed and agitated. Someone honks at you in traffic; someone steps ahead of you in line—work on seeing life's small irritations as opportunities to practice patience. You'll develop a skill you can employ when you really need it, like the middle of an argument with your spouse.

Make time for developing a practice.

Developing the ability to improve your behavior doesn't happen overnight. It's a *practice*, like learning a musical instrument, and requires regular effort. Dedicate some small area of your living space (even a corner of a room will do) as a fixed meditation spot, and dedicate some time to daily sitting, even if it's just five minutes to start.

Study how your mind works, and practice taming it through meditation.

Generally, we're ruled by our wishes, likes, and dislikes. Through meditation and contemplation, you'll gain a deeper sense of how these thoughts rise up. Most importantly, you'll develop the ability to let them fall away before they lead to agitation and unfortunate action. Work to recognize the unspoken thoughts that lie behind your feelings—and to let go of the ones that lead you to suffer.

Practice meditation to gain a wider view.

In fights with our partner, we tend to say, "You *always* do x." One goal of meditation is to strip ourselves of such crusty pre-conceptions, and to locate Shunryu Suzuki's fresh beginner's mind. It's a practice designed to bring our attention to the moment, to what *is* now; to help us let go of what we think things might be, or wish they were. In any situation in which you're inclined to jump to a conclusion about why your partner is behaving a certain way, try telling yourself: *not necessarily so.*

Gather all blames into one.

This core Buddhist saying means that, instead of blaming our difficulties on all sorts of external people and situations, we need to recognize that the chief cause of our suffering is within our own mind: it comes from our distorted way of thinking about things. Once we see this, we can take responsibility for our own suffering and happiness.

Use meditation to increase your compassion.

Think about how your partner is really just like you: someone who wants to avoid suffering and be happy. Contemplate how your relationship might change if you work on seeing their needs as more pressing than your own. Practice taking and giving: imagine that you are breathing in their suffering as dark smoke, and that you are breathing out (toward them) a blissful clear light. (The point is not that this will have some magical effect on them in that moment, but that it will ease your own troubled heart and help you behave in a more compassionate way.)

Find teachers and guides.

It's best if you can find someone to learn from directly—
Buddhism places a lot of emphasis on personal teaching—
but if you live far from Buddhist centers or classes, many
books and magazines can help. (Please see the appendix for
suggestions).

Seek out others who will support your practice.

The incredible success of AA is largely predicated on the fact
that it's based around support from fellow members. Likewise, the spiritual path is made a lot easier with the help of
friends who can empathize with your frustrations, encourage
your efforts, and provide insight into your questions.
Chances are good that you'll encounter people who came to
Buddhism for the same reason you did: they're also seeking
to learn how to deal with painful life issues such as a divorce
or other loss.

Contemplate the difference between
real love and attachment.

Real love says, "I have a passion to be loving." Attachment
says, "I have a passion to be loved." Real love says, "I want
you to be happy." Attachment says, "I need you to make me
happy." When both partners are concerned with the other's
happiness, you create a healthy loop that feeds itself. When
both partners are concerned primarily with what they can
get from the relationship, you have a recipe for failure. Sort
your feelings to discover which are founded in love and
which are driven by attachment. Helpful hint: if your mind
feels very agitated, you're probably suffering from desirous
attachment.

Resolve to forgive your partner.

This doesn't necessarily mean that you excuse the wrongs they might have done you. It *does* mean that you understand that those wrongs arose out of delusional minds, not inherent bad nature. It means you reconnect with your partner's complicated humanity, and recognize that they are a suffering being, just like you. You can't take this compassionate step until you feel ready, but when you do, you'll find that setting down the burden of your anger and resentment will lighten your own load.

Exercise.

Not a Buddhist instruction, per se, but physical exercise is enormously helpful for relieving stress, burning off bad moods, and generally improving your sense of well-being and confidence.

Reflect on impermanence and change.

Through direct observation and through meditation, work on appreciating that nothing in the universe stays the same. A marriage is no exception. Understand that your partner cannot always match your initial, idealized image of them. People are bound to change over time, and we need to be prepared to accept that. Work to let go of your disappointment that your marriage was not permanent, and to become more accepting of your divorce as a manifestation of change.

Work on increasing empathy and compassion.

Practice empathy by striving to see everyone, including your partner, as if they were yourself. Practice compassion by striving to treat everyone, including your partner, as if they were an enlightened being. Work on ridding your thoughts and speech of negativity and criticism. Don't dwell on your partner's hurtful behavior as it relates to you; meditate instead on how it arises from their own suffering.

Work on letting go of self-cherishing.

When your mind gets agitated about a certain situation, dig deep and you will often discover that your sense of self-importance, that insistent *What about me?*, is at the root of the problem. In conflicts with your partner, strive to take your wishes and desires out of the equation, so you can hear what they are saying.

Practice generosity.

This is a great antidote to the self-cherishing that gets us in so much trouble. Give more to charity, but also practice generosity in other ways: by volunteering, by making more of an effort to help friends and family, by giving respect and acknowledgment to everyone you meet—and by seeing when you can surrender victories to your partner for the sake of greater harmony.

Reflect on emptiness.

Contemplate the fact that nobody has a fixed identity, and work on giving up your attachment to stories about what kind of person you are, what kind of person your partner is. Consider that you might be wrong. Strive to give up your fierce attachment to the way you want the world to be. Lighten up!

Be kind.

As the Dalai Lama says, it all really comes down to this simple two-word prescription. It's essential to do no harm, but this takes matters a great step further. In any difficult moment with your partner, ask yourself, *Am I being kind? If not, what would be the kind thing to do in this situation?* Buddhist practice can contain many different elements and aspects, but this fundamental precept will always steer you right.

a buddhist approach
to divorce, in action

Before we wrap things up, let's take one more look at how to apply all of these steps to a specific situation. Let's say that you've been divorced for a year, and you and your spouse have joint custody of a child. One day, you come home to a voice mail saying that your ex will not be able to take his or her scheduled turn as caretaker next weekend. You don't have any major plans for the weekend, but you're not at all happy about this violation of your custody agreement. (Or let's reverse the message—let's say you're looking forward to having the kids next weekend, but your ex wants to take them out of town. Imagine whatever pushes the anger button for you.)

Let's look at several different ways this might play out.

Scenario One: Anger

You feel a flare of anger. You immediately reach for the phone and have the following conversation:

YOU: I just got your message. What's going on?

YOUR EX: I know it's my weekend to take care of Junior, but there's a work conference I'd really like to—

YOU: That's not my problem. We went through all of that crap with the lawyers, and we made an agreement.

YOUR EX: I know that, but it's not going to kill you to just cut me a little slack for once . . .

YOU: This is *your* problem, not mine.

YOUR EX: Why can't you just be nice, for once?

YOU: For once? You always blame me for [continued, in an irate vein . . .]

◖

Yikes. Not a very productive conversation, and certainly not a pleasant one. It starts with anger, and gets worse.

Let's stop and ask a major question here: *What's my ultimate goal in this interaction?*

There are a number of possible options:

1) I want to get revenge on my spouse for all of the suffering he/she has caused me. (Petty, yes, but divorce has a way of bringing out small-mindedness in even the most saintly of us.)

2) This is a battle, and I'm gonna win.

Since you've stuck with this book so far, I trust you'll see the folly of these options. As we just witnessed, those approaches are just pouring gasoline on a fire. They'll make matters worse in the future—not only for your spouse, but for you as well.

Let's try another goal:

3) I want *justice*—an equitable resolution of this particular situation.

Scenario Two: Justice

You feel a flare of anger. You take a few deep breaths, pace around a bit until you calm down, and then reach for the phone.

YOU: I just got your message. I'll tell you what: I'll make a deal with you. I'll take Junior this weekend if you take him on my next scheduled weekend.

YOUR EX: [After a pause] Well, I guess that's fair. All right—thanks.

That went a lot better, right? It seems perfectly reasonable and rational and free from destructive feelings or actions. It's *fair*.

Answer Three is tricky, though. What's wrong with it?

For one thing, this approach tends to encourage a tit-for-tat mentality. *I'm not going to do something kind, because my spouse wasn't kind to me in our last conflict. I'm not going to be generous, because I'm going to match his/her lack of generosity.*

That doesn't have to happen, though, and this approach might work if you want to settle for a limited, temporary improvement in your relationship with your ex. But if you want to actually *transform* the situation—to bring a truly positive change into both of your lives, you can decide to take things a step further. You can aspire to a higher goal:

4) I want to positively transform my relationship with my ex, not just in this situation, but in general. I want to end up happier, *and* I want my ex to end up happier.

Scenario Three: A Buddhist Approach

You feel a flare of anger. You recognize how strong it is, and realize that there might be destructive consequences if you react quickly. You resolve to meditate in order to calm down, and to figure out why you feel so deeply agitated.

At first, you just sit for a few minutes, noticing the tension in your shoulders, the hot feeling in your chest, the way your hands want to clench. You breathe deeply, relaxing your body, imagining your agitation flowing away like dark smoke with each breath.

When some of your tension has slipped away and your breathing grows more calm and even, you turn to some contemplation. *Why am I so pissed off? Does my level of upset match the situation in front of me? (I didn't have any big plans for this weekend, so am I really going to be so inconvenienced?) What's the real root of my anger?*

You dig deeper, and discover—surprise, surprise—that you're angry because you feel like an injustice is being done to you. In other words, you're hearing that strong inner voice crying out, *What about me?* You begin to question what might happen if you could release that tight, panicky grip on your sense of outraged self.

You dig deeper still. *Is my ex really doing this because they want to hurt me? Maybe—but not necessarily so. Maybe I'm imputing motives that are simply not there. Maybe this is not really about me at all. Perhaps my ex genuinely just wants to go to this conference to improve his/her career situation. Maybe that will ultimately be beneficial for our child. Maybe it will improve the overall financial picture for all three of us.*

This contemplation helps, but you still feel remnants of anger. You take a step back, look at a bigger picture. *This situation certainly feels like a problem, but maybe I can look at it in a different way. I'm trying to become more patient, less angry, less agitated, more kind—and life has just presented me with a great opportunity to practice. I can look at it as an experiment: What will happen if I try to apply the new insights I've learned?*

You settle into your cushion, and dig deeper still. What if you stopped worrying about what you'll get out of the situation, and try focusing on your ex? You spend a few minutes reflecting on how your ex is—like you—just acting out of a desire to avoid suffering and find happiness. You imagine that you're breathing in their suffering as dark smoke, and that you're breathing toward them a blissful clear light. After a while, you start to genuinely feel more compassion, and a true wish to help them out.

You open your eyes. You pick up the phone.

YOU: I just got your message. Since this conference sounds important to you, I'll be glad to take Junior this weekend.

YOUR EX: [stunned] Really?

YOU: Yeah. I hope you have a good conference.

YOUR EX: You're not kidding?

YOU: Nope.

YOUR EX: You're not angry?

YOU: Nope.

YOUR EX: That's it?

YOU: Yep.

Period. (No angry confrontation, no negotiation.)

Let's review:

In the first scenario, both you and your ex walked away angrier and unhappier than before.

In the second scenario, you might have improved your relationship a little, but you didn't change the status quo very much. No big gains in happiness for either party.

And in the third scenario? Well, your *ex* is probably walking away happier. They got what they wanted, with no argument and no fuss.

And you?

The voice of logic intervenes. *You just got robbed!* You're going to end up doing something you're not thrilled about, and you didn't get anything tangible in return. And what if your spouse sees your giving in as a sign that she/he can take advantage of your newfound generosity in the future?

First of all, the point is not that you should end up behaving like a doormat. If your spouse consistently comes up with excuses, you're certainly entitled to (calmly) point that out, and to be firm about their need to hold up their end of your joint parental responsibilities.

In the meantime, though, let's take a longer view, and use a higher logic. What did you get out of this interchange? First of all, you can be justly proud that you didn't act out of anger or vindictiveness. You got to free yourself from some self-cherishing anxiety, and to experience the lightness of heart that generosity brings. Maybe you helped change your spouse's vision of you. (It's easy for them to feel justified in battling someone they perceive as an adversary, but how long can they hold onto their anger if they're confronted with kindness?) Maybe your next contact will be less tense. Maybe they'll help you out when you need it. You just pumped some positive energy into the loop of your relationship, and ultimately that's likely to come around and benefit you.

To benefit both of you.

And your child.

And your families and friends and the people around you.

Nobody has to lose.

Everybody wins.

buddhist resources

Helpful Books

NOTE: There are many books about Buddhism available today, with topics ranging from Buddhism and motherhood to Zen and golf. This is a list of some books that I happened to come across that were useful to me. It's not meant to be comprehensive — I have certainly left out many worthwhile books and authors, and I have included several authors who are not Buddhists at all. Many of the authors mentioned have published a number of excellent books; I've included just one, and hope that reading it might lead you to the others.

Good books to start with

Beck, Charlotte Joko. *Everyday Zen: Love and Work*. San Francisco: HarperOne, 2007.

The Best Buddhist Writing, Edited by Melvin McLeod and the editors of *Shambhala Sun.* Boston: Shambhala Publications, annual publication.

Chödrön, Pema. *When Things Fall Apart: Heart Advice for Difficult Times.* Boston: Shambhala Publications, 1997.

His Holiness TheDalai Lama and Howard C. Cutler MD. *The Art of Happiness.* New York: Riverhead Books, 1998.

Epstein, Mark. *Going to Pieces Without Falling Apart: A Buddhist Perspective on Wholeness.* New York: Broadway Books, 1999.

Gyatso, Geshe Kelsang. *Transform Your Life: A Blissful Journey.* Glen Spey, NY: Tharpa Publications, 2001.

Kabat-Zinn, Jon. *Wherever You Go, There You Are: Mindfulness Meditation in Everyday Life.* New York: Hyperion, 2005.

Nhat Hanh, Thich. *Anger.* New York: Riverhead Books, 2002.

Rizzetto, Diane Eshin. *Waking Up to What You Do.* Boston: Shambhala Publications, 2006.

Rosenberg, Larry. *Breath by Breath: The Liberating Practice of Insight Meditation.* Boston: Shambhala Publications, 2004.

Smedes, Lewis B. *Forgive and Forget: Healing the Hurts We Don't Deserve.* San Francisco: HarperOne, 2007.

Smith, Jean. *The Beginner's Guide to Zen Buddhism.* New York: Bell Tower/Random House, 2000.

Tannen, Deborah. *You Just Don't Understand: Women and Men in Conversation.* New York: Harper Paperbacks, 2001.

Other helpful books

Armstrong, Karen. *Buddha.* New York: Penguin Putnam, Inc., 2004.

Batchelor, Stephen. *Buddhism Without Beliefs.* New York: Tricycle/Riverhead, 1997.

Becker, Ernest. *The Denial of Death*. New York: Free Press, 1973.

Begley, Sharon. *Train Your Mind, Change Your Brain: How a New Science Reveals Our Extraordinary Potential to Transform Ourselves*. New York: Ballantine Books, 2007.

Boorstein, Sylvia. *Pay Attention for Goodness Sake*. New York: Ballantine Books, 2003.

Das, Lama Surya. *Awakening the Buddha Within: Tibetan Wisdom for the Western World*. New York: Broadway Books, 1997.

Gilbert, Daniel. *Stumbling On Happiness*. New York: Alfred A. Knopf, 2006.

Goldberg, Natalie. *Long Quiet Highway: Waking Up in America*. New York: Bantam Dell, 1994.

Gray, John. *Men Are from Mars, Women Are from Venus: The Classic Guide to Understanding the Opposite Sex*. New York: Harper-Collins Publishers, 1992.

Hagen, Steve. *Buddhism Is Not What You Think: Finding Freedom Beyond Beliefs*. San Francisco: HarperOne, 2004.

Jeon, Arthur. *City Dharma: Keeping Your Cool in the Chaos*. New York: Harmony Books, 2004.

Hooked! Buddhist Writings on Greed, Desire, and the Urge to Consume. Edited by Stephanie Kaza. Boston: Shambhala Publications, 2005.

Kornfield, Jack. *After the Ecstasy, the Laundry: How the Heart Grows Wise on the Spiritual Path*. New York: Bantam Dell, 2001.

Levine, Noah. *Dharma Punx: A Memoir*. San Francisco: Harper-SanFrancisco, 2003.

Mipham, Sakyong. *Turning the Mind Into An Ally*. New York: Riverhead Books, 2004.

Moore, Dinty W. *The Accidental Buddhist: Mindfulness, Enlightenment, and Sitting Still, American Style*. New York: Main Street Books, 1999.

Pine, Jeffery. *Re-Enchantment: Tibetan Buddhism Comes to the West*. New York: W. W. Norton, 2004.

Ricard, Matthieu. *Happiness: A Guide to Developing Life's Most Important Skill*. New York: Little, Brown and Company, 2007.

Roach, Geshe Michael. *The Diamond Cutter: The Buddha on Managing Your Business and Your Life*. New York: Doubleday, 2000.

Salzberg, Sharon. *A Heart As Wide As the World: Stories on the Path of Lovingkindness*. Boston: Shambhala Publications, 1999.

Shantideva. *The Way of the Bodhisattva*. Boston: Shambhala Publications, 2003.

Snow, Kimberley. *In Buddha's Kitchen: Cooking, Being Cooked, and Other Adventures in a Meditation Center*. Boston: Shambhala Publications, 2004.

Sutin, Lawrence. *All Is Change: The Two-Thousand-Year Journey of Buddhism to the West*. New York: Little, Brown and Company, 2006.

Suzuki, D. T., and Carl Jung. *An Introduction to Zen Buddhism*. New York: Grove Press, 1994.

Suzuki, Shunryu. *Zen Mind, Beginner's Mind*. Boston: Shambhala Publications, 2006.

Thomas, Claude Anshin. *At Hell's Gate: A Soldier's Journey From War to Peace*. Boston: Shambhala Publications, 2006.

Thurman, Robert. *Infinite Life: Awakening to Bliss Within*. New York: Riverhead, 2005.

Trungpa, Chögyam. *Cutting Through Spiritual Materialism*. Boston: Shambhala Publications, 2002.

Wallis, Glenn. *Basic Teachings of the Buddha*. New York: Modern Library, 2007.

Magazines

Shambhala Sun, www.Shambhalasun.com, 1-877-786-1950 ext. 10
Tricycle: The Buddhist Review, www.Tricycle.com

Buddhist Centers

There are many Buddhist centers around the world; to find ones close to you, search online or check out the listings in the back of magazines such as *Shambhala Sun*.

acknowledgments

This book was literally made possible by the kindness of many people.

First of all, I would like to thank some friends whose great kindness and compassion helped me survive my divorce. I am eternally grateful to Tim Cross and Tracy Agerton, James Chew, Gina and Warren Katz, Karen Graham and Dan Ilian, Blake Nelson, and Roxanne Aubrey.

I am enormously grateful to Chakrasambara Buddhist Center and its excellent teachers who introduced me to the Buddhist path, including Geshe Kelsang Gyatso, Kadam Morten, Gen-la Dekyong, and Matthew Riechers. Thanks also to Kelsang Jampa of Vajradakini Buddhist Center. My explanations of Buddhist insights owe a huge debt to their clear, incisive presentations. Thanks likewise to the many superb writers on Buddhism mentioned in the resources. Any errors are my own.

Thanks to a multitude of insightful and kind fellow practitioners and friends, especially to the Park Slope Foundation Program class, and those who so generously shared their inspiring personal stories.

Thanks to a number of wise and helpful readers of portions or the whole of this manuscript, including Stefan Forbes, Tim Cockey, Miriam Cohen, Matthew Riechers, S. J. Rozan, Lucinda Rogers, and Karen Graham.

Thanks to Dr. Judith Lee (who proved how therapy could be very helpful), to Sifu Jared Cooper (tai chi teacher extraordinaire), Uli Baer (for friendship and helpful advice), Patrick Jennings (for extraordinary understanding), Elaine Breeden and Elizabeth Ely (for early exposure to wider ideas), Lori Ann Caraballo (a true and wise pal), Erin Stratford (who inspires me with her patience and compassion), Sunny Balzano (for his shining example of how to be a friend to the world), Beth Ann Bovino (for valuable lessons), David Harshada Wagner (for excellent teachings on how to meditate), Dr. Tara Goodrich (for explaining that I *don't* have antisocial personality disorder), Sifu Shi Yan Ming of USA Shaolin Temple (for teaching me how to "eat bitter"), and my poker pals (VV, K-Ro, Sir William of McKenna, the Lady Diane, Captain Sacha, and TKO), for general good friendliness and for teaching me that money is also impermanent.

Grateful thanks to my hard-working agent, Anna Ghosh, who believed in this book from the beginning and made it happen. And a very special thanks to the amazing crew at Da Capo press, including Cisca Schreefel, Lindsey Lochner, Lindsey Triebel, Trent Knoss, and—above all—my editor, Renée Sedliar, who utterly disproved the notion that "editors don't edit anymore" with her sensitive, detailed, and enormously helpful suggestions.

May everyone be happy and free from suffering.